LLEWELLYN'S

Little Book of

HALLOWEEN

Brittany Sherman

Mickie Mueller (Missouri) explores magic and spirituality through art and the written word. She includes magical herbal washes in her art that correspond with the subject, making every piece enchanted. She is the author/illustrator of *The Voice of the Trees*, the illustrator of *Mystical Cats Tarot*, the cocreator of *Magical Dogs Tarot*, and author of *The Witch's Mirror*. Her art has been seen as set dressing on SyFy's *The Magicians* and Bravo's *Girlfriend's Guide to Divorce*. Visit her online at www.MickieMuellerArt.com.

LLEWELLYN'S
Little Book of
HALLOWEEN

MICKIE MUELLER

LLEWELLYN PUBLICATIONS
WOODBURY, MINNESOTA

FIRST EDITION
Second Printing, 2019

Book design by Rebecca Zins
Cover cartouche by Freepik
Cover design by Lisa Novak and Shira Atakpu

Llewellyn Publications is a registered trademark of Llewellyn Worldwide Ltd.

Library of Congress Cataloging-in-Publication Data

Names: Mueller, Mickie, author. | Llewellyn Publications, editor.
Title: Llewellyn's little book of Halloween / Mickie Mueller.
Other titles: Little book of Halloween
Description: First edition. | Woodbury, Minnesota : Llewellyn Publications, 2018. | Includes bibliographical references.
Identifiers: LCCN 2018020610 (print) | LCCN 2018021540 (ebook) | ISBN 9780738758305 (ebook) | ISBN 9780738758213 (alk. paper)
Subjects: LCSH: Halloween.
Classification: LCC BF1572.H35 (ebook) | LCC BF1572.H35 M84 2018 (print) | DDC 394.2646—dc22
LC record available at https://lccn.loc.gov/2018020610

Llewellyn Publications
A Division of Llewellyn Worldwide Ltd.
2143 Wooddale Drive
Woodbury, MN 55125-2989
www.llewellyn.com

Printed in China

To Lisa, charter member and cofounder
of the Witch's Club, for being a great friend,
sharing in Halloween magic, and helping
me keep my childhood weird.

Also to Robin, who put up with a slightly
scary sister all those years. Sorry about
those triffids. I love you!

Contents

Exercises

Tips

ACKNOWLEDGMENTS

A big thanks to Bill Krause for bringing me on for this project; what great fun we've had with this. Thanks to Becky Zins for being a keen-eyed editor and brilliant book designer; you always make my books look great. Thanks to my family—Dan, Tristan, Brittany, Chelsea, Mom, Dad, Robin, and Sandy—for great Halloween memories and for always being on board with my various Halloween-related shenanigans. Thanks to Blake for insight when I ran a few things by you. A warm thanks to the whole team at Llewellyn for all they do every step of the way.

INTRODUCTION

When I was a kid, my family always said, "If Mickie could have anything she wanted for Christmas, it would be Halloween!" Of course, that was true. As I sit here writing this it's October 1, the leaves are changing, the pumpkin harvest is in, and every trip to the store ends with the phrase "Do you want to check out the Halloween aisle?" answered by grins and nods of approval. For me—and probably for you since you have this book in your hands—this is truly the most magical time of the year!

1

The first Halloween I recall was the year I thought the profession of ballerina was a completely valid career path for me. Even though it later became apparent for so many reasons that this was not going to happen, I got to be an actual ballerina that night. I wore an embroidered coat over the top of my gorgeous tulle-and-satin flower ballerina costume that had been handcrafted by my mom, and we ventured into the streets of our neighborhood.

This was the early 1970s, when we all waited until sundown; then, gripping our plastic pumpkins and pillowcases, in droves we descended on the neighborhood to gather our bounty. Back then most of it was prepackaged candy, but we still got the occasional homemade treat such as popcorn balls or caramel apples. There were also those weird candies wrapped in black and orange waxed paper. (What the heck were those?) Such good times!

Houses back then were decorated with glowing jack-o'-lanterns and hinged paper figures of witches and ghosts taped to the windows, and that was about it. Occasionally there would be someone who would really take it to the next level, though, like the couple who lived a few streets down. One of the guys would dress up like the

We all felt the power of transformation and anonymity while wearing our Halloween costumes.

Wicked Witch of the West and run around on the roof cackling and tossing candy down to the kids below while his partner kept his candy stocked with occasional trips up the ladder. Those guys made our Halloween!

As I got older I tried out many costumes and personas. Some were gorgeous homemade creations while others were the terrible plastic masks and vinyl smocks from the store with a picture on the front so people knew who the heck you were supposed to be. Either way, we all felt the power of transformation and anonymity while wearing our Halloween costumes.

There was always something else about Halloween, though. I was a kid, so of course the candy was great and

As scared as we were, it was fun
to face our fear. The rush we
got from overcoming that fear
was empowering, like we had
looked into the actual realm of
spirits and faced a real danger,
coming out triumphant.

who doesn't love dressing up, but there was always an otherworldly element that I felt behind the usual trappings of the day. Even as a kid I could feel it in the air—this time wasn't only fun, it was somehow significant, powerful. I remember thinking about the colors of Halloween, black and orange, and awaiting the setting sun against the trees as I noticed those colors there in nature on Halloween. Occasionally I would dream of primeval spirits that seemed out of place in the everyday world. The air in the weeks leading up to Halloween felt electric to me; I felt a shift before I knew what that even meant, as if something much more ancient was coming through.

I stopped trick-or-treating at an earlier age than many of my friends, but I have never given up Halloween. The last year I recall going out to get candy was with my best friend, Lisa; I think we were in sixth grade. We were both dressed as witches, and her dad made up our faces with burnt cork, adding wrinkles and lines to look like crones. We were delighted!

Most houses were still decorated with only pumpkins, but there was one house that terrified us. Scary music was playing loudly from inside, and when they opened the door there were two threatening ghostly figures who answered. Several black lights glowed in the doorway, lighting up these spirits with a paranormal luminescence, and strobe lights gave the scene a surreal quality. Only the bravest kids held up their plastic pumpkin buckets at arm's length as they quaked and trembled, poised to run away screaming as soon as the hard-earned candy bars were dropped in.

We looked at each other and debated whether it was worth it. Then we realized that tonight we weren't two of the shyest girls in the sixth grade, we were witches, and scary ones at that. We screwed up our courage, summoned up our inner witches, and marched right up to that door. We left with more than just candy that night. As scared as we were, it was fun to face our fear. The rush we got from overcoming that fear was empowering, like we had looked into the actual realm of spirits and faced a real danger, coming out triumphant.

After that Halloween, we vowed that we would hand out treats together from the scariest house on the block. I hope that some of the kids who braved our house of terror year after year got that same feeling. Who would have guessed that my costume that year, unlike the ballerina, would be representative of my future spiritual path and career choice that was years away but always dancing on the edges of Halloween?

In high school I remember making up an invitation for a party I was having and summing up a brief description of the party as "All Hallows' Eve, known as Samhain in ancient times..." Having done a bit of research on the history of Halloween, I thought it was interesting and added an air of mystery to my invitations. Little did I know at the time that Samhain was the reason I had felt something stirring in the air in October since childhood, and it would become an important part of my spiritual practice later in life.

Years went by, and every home I lived in I considered how it would look decked out for Halloween. In time, I was taking my own kids out trick-or-treating. I even worked both designing and acting in a couple local haunted houses when my kids were older. My favorite was a small one in an indoor mall in St. Louis that was run for charity to help a local Catholic children's home. My roommate and fellow artist Sandy and I designed a lot of that haunted house; we were introduced to the sister in charge by a friend who was making a video for the project. I'll tell you, you haven't lived until a nun has asked you if you have enough plastic flies for the *Amityville Horror* room or if you need more!

My daughters acted as shills, standing in line with the other patrons and talking about how scared they were to go in. When my kids came through, we would all giggle, then Sandy (in costume) would follow my daughters out the exit and grab them, dragging them back in as the girls put on a show of kicking and screaming for the next group in line. Yeah, we were a bit like the Addams Family, but we raised a lot of money for that children's home!

Many people have shared some similar Halloween experiences with me, and as I've recently discovered some even share some of my Samhain experiences as well, noticing from childhood that there was something more to Halloween than candy and costumes.

In the '90s I found my spiritual path and discovered the ways of natural magic that flows through the air, lives in the trees, and is part of us all. I began to do my research into the subjects of Wicca, Paganism, and the craft of the

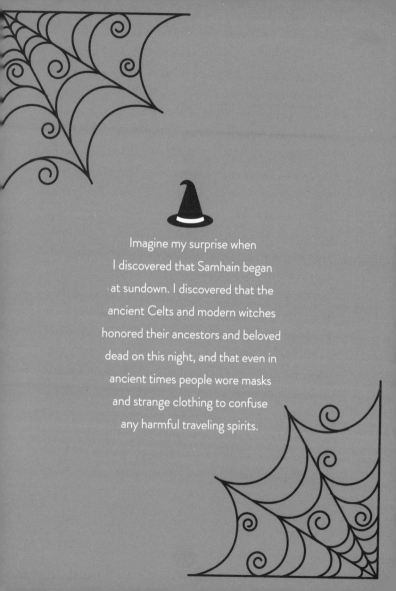

Imagine my surprise when
I discovered that Samhain began
at sundown. I discovered that the
ancient Celts and modern witches
honored their ancestors and beloved
dead on this night, and that even in
ancient times people wore masks
and strange clothing to confuse
any harmful traveling spirits.

modern witch, and I found them to be steeped in and inspired by older traditions, much like Halloween is. I learned about the eight sabbats of the Pagans of old, among them Samhain, which by no mere coincidence falls on the modern secular holiday known as Halloween. The odd feeling of energy in the air on Halloween that I'd noticed all my life was real? Oh yes, it was real, all right, and there was more.

Samhain was a festival that rang in the Celtic New Year, and when did it begin? Imagine my surprise when I discovered that Samhain began at sundown. I discovered that the ancient Celts and modern witches honored their ancestors and beloved dead on this night, and that even in ancient times people wore masks and strange clothing to confuse any harmful traveling spirits. It was the season when the veil between the world of the living and the world of spirits and fae was at its thinnest. Food, bonfires, and drinking were all part of this very old celebration. All these ancient traditions had somehow been carried down through the ages right to us and become part of our lives. Learning all of this was a revelation.

I now celebrate both Halloween and Samhain; I decorate my house and my altar. I hand out candy to children and make offerings to my ancestors. I carve jack-o'-lanterns to impress and invite trick-or-treaters, and I also enchant them to ward my home from mischief both mortal and spiritual. I wear a costume because it's fun and because it reminds me of my spiritual ancestors, who used costumes for protection and spiritual transformation just the way two sixth-grade witches did all those years ago. I light candles for both mood and magic. I fill my house with the music of Halloween and the cleansing smoke of incense and sage. It is said that witches walk between two worlds, and never has that been truer than during Halloween and Samhain.

Come along with me and walk between the worlds. Let's peer beyond the veil together and explore the mystical place where the modern secular holiday of Halloween and the ancient festival of the dead known as Samhain meet and mingle on one magical night. Whether you celebrate Halloween, Samhain, or both, we'll have a great time and learn a thing or two along the way about this mystical season.

one

HALLOWEEN
THROUGHOUT
HISTORY

When we think of Halloween, we think of it as being a modern holiday with a huge commercial presence, with store aisles and even entire pop-up stores devoted to costumes, decorations, and partyware. On the surface it looks like a holiday invented by candy companies and the manufacturers of Styrofoam tombstones, but the commercialization of Halloween is only a recent addition to the holiday. The truth is, Halloween is full of traditions and practices that go back at least 2,500 years;

some archeological evidence suggests maybe as far as 5,000 years. Throughout history there have been efforts to stamp out the holiday by renaming it, co-opting it, or just straight-up forbidding it, but it was the feast day of the dead that just wouldn't die.

Halloween's Agricultural Link

Let's explore the roots of Halloween and learn more about how the traditions were born and evolved over the years. Imagine going back in time over 2,000 years ago to the lands of the Celts in the British Isles and France. We know from medieval texts that they celebrated this time of year throughout the lands; it was probably originally a three-day festival celebrated during the time that fell right between the autumn equinox and the winter solstice. The Druids kept track of the astronomical events and seasons, using that information to mark time throughout the year. The oldest written records of this Pagan festival were from the early Middle Ages, when it was celebrated on October 31. No one knows when that date was settled on, but it likely came about when the Georgian calendar was introduced.

No matter the calendar date or astronomical date, the ancient Celts didn't call it Halloween; they called it Samhain (pronounced SAH-win). Some scholars have interpreted the word Samhain to mean "summer's end," others suggest the word meant "an assembly" or "gathering," but we do know it was one of the harvest festivals, the last one of the year. In a society that counted on agriculture and livestock, the people recognized more than one harvest because it didn't happen all at the same time; it's more of a process. Cold days were coming, and there was no running down to the corner store for stuff to make for dinner. They had to make do with whatever they had and hope it lasted through winter.

By Samhain they had brought in the last of the bounty from the fields to store. The excess livestock was being slaughtered for food; only the minimum needed to breed in the spring would be kept through the winter. The people were preparing for the hardest time of the year, and as life was leaving the land their thoughts turned toward the nature of mortality. They felt the doors to the Otherworld shift open; their ancestors were close, and so were other wandering spirits known as the sídhe or faeries—

but we're not talking Tinker Bell here. These were old primal spirits who could mess up your whole situation if they were inclined to do so.

People travelled through the community gathering up firewood and food for the feast. As they went door to door they wore primitive masks, face paint, and disguises to trick the fae or any dark spirits that may be roaming into leaving them be. It was not "trick-or-treat" but more "trick and survive the ghosts and spirits of the land"!

The fires of all the households were extinguished before the main celebration fire was lit. This bonfire, also known as a needfire, contained wood from nine sacred trees and was lit by friction; later, a branch or embers from the Samhain needfire would be brought back to the homes to reignite each hearth, bringing the homes of the community together with the flame of the communal fire.

Festivals for the Beloved Dead

Even though people were thinking of their beloved dead, this was a celebration. The Celts didn't consider death to be evil; instead, they considered it to be part of life. There was feasting and celebrating abundance, however temporary it might be. This was also the beginning of the Celts' New Year—as they put the old year behind them they repaid debts, took care of taxes, and there is evidence that they also got pretty drunk. Divination was also performed at Samhain; being the New Year, everyone wanted some insight into what lay ahead during the harsh winter and how abundant the next year might be.

Meanwhile, in Rome the Pagans there were honoring the dead during a different time of the year: May 9, 11, and 13. Lemuria was a festival of the dead when ghosts or dark spirits known as lemures wandered the earth. These were considered angry spirits of the deceased who hadn't had proper Roman burials or ancestral spirits from the underworld. This was a somber festival during which the vengeful spirits were exorcised from homes by the head of the household, who offered black beans as appeasement and clanged bronze pots together to drive them away. Now, you may be asking what a festival of the dead in May has to do with Halloween? Bear with me; it will all make sense.

First of all, it is notable that the Celtic celebration of Beltane is the opposite of Samhain on the astronomical calendar. Beltane falls in early May, smack between the spring equinox and the summer solstice, and is the other time of the year when the borders to the spirit world are considered to be open. It's very close to the dates that the Romans celebrated Lemuria; it could be a coincidence, but I wanted to point it out.

In 609 CE Pope Boniface IV was working to convert all the Roman Pagans to Christianity, knowing that allowing people to keep their current popular traditions and adjusting those practices to make them Christian was much easier than getting people to stop celebrating their festival days altogether. This method was used to great effect in the Christianization of many Pagan Europeans throughout history. The pope reconsecrated the Pagan temple known as the Pantheon at Rome to the Virgin Mary and the Christian martyrs, and what date did he choose for this big dedication? He scheduled it on May

13, of course: the last day of Lemuria. Soon Lemuria was dubbed All Saints' Day. Instead of being concerned with the dead spirits wandering the earth, the newly converted Christians were directed to venerate the dead martyred Christian saints as a sanctioned substitute. So originally All Saints' Day was added to the calendar to keep newly converted Romans from celebrating Lemuria, an early May festival of the dead.

In the British Isles during the Middle Ages, the church's efforts to win ground was having some success converting people to Christianity by convincing the locals that their nature deities were actually evil. The people of the outlying rural areas including Ireland, Scotland, and the Isle of Mann still had not given up celebrating Samhain, much to the chagrin of the church. Pope Gregory III, realizing that old habits die hard, decided to move All Saints' Day from May to November 1. The similar themes of Lumeria and Samhain were now to be assimilated into the Christian celebration of All Saints' Day. Another name for it was All Hallows' Day or Hallowmas because hallow meant holy, and it was the day of the holies. The day before All Hallows' Day, October 31, became known as

All Hallows' Evening or Eve, and eventually through the ages became shortened to Halloween, the name we use for the holiday today.

The introduction of All Saints' Day and later All Souls' Day was eventually adopted by many but with some of the original cultural traditions surviving in different forms. All Souls' Day was added November 2 and designated as a day to honor the departed Christian souls. This was an attempt to redirect the Pagan practices still being recognized on All Hallows' Eve that the people still hadn't abandoned, such as remembering their own departed. This move was meant to strengthen the church's hold on the fall festival of the dead.

All Souls' Day was a day of prayer for the dead, especially those who were believed to be stuck in purgatory, which was the halfway point between heaven and hell according to Christian beliefs; I like to imagine a long line at the spiritual DMV—no one in purgatory was having any fun. The belief was that prayers for these souls would elevate them into heaven.

Children and the poor began a practice called "Souling" on All Souls' Day. They would travel door to door offering prayers for the dead in exchange for small cakes

Trick or treat
or anything sweet!

flavored with spices, dried fruit, and sometimes saffron. The cakes were marked with an equal-armed cross and called soul cakes. Soulers would sometimes recite poems asking for soul cakes or "anything sweet" in exchange for prayers. Was this the beginning of the modern tradition of trick-or-treat?

The First Jack-o'-Lanterns

Regarding souls who couldn't get into heaven, a cautionary tale arose about a man called "Stingy Jack," who was such a jerk he couldn't get into heaven or hell and was doomed to walk the earth with a carved turnip lantern. In areas like Ireland and Scotland people hollowed out turnips or large beets and carved faces in them. These small effigies were lit from within with a glowing coal or candle stump and placed near gates and doorways to welcome spirits of loved ones and frighten off any dark spirits that might pass by. These spooky lanterns mimicked the one carried by Stingy Jack and were the first jack-o'-lanterns. The jack-o'-lantern would eventually become the most iconic symbol of Halloween. (More on Stingy Jack's story and the meaning behind other classical Halloween symbols will follow in chapter 2.)

Other uses for these lanterns through the ages included using them to scare or prank others as they could be mistaken for will-o'-the-wisps (a kind of fae light) or ghosts—after all, a night of spirits is the perfect time to scare someone. Turnips and manglewerzels (beets) are still carved in some areas of Ireland, Scotland, Germany, and Sweden to this day.

The tradition of Souling on All Souls' Day eventually included guising or mumming, another earlier practice brought into the cities from the rural Pagan communities. Carrying their lanterns and gathering in the streets, costumed revelers performed short plays or other performances. In return, the residents offered food or money for their entertainment. It was considered great fun, but the celebration of old Samhain and new Halloween was about to be caught right in the middle of a battle of religion and politics.

The power of the Catholic Church grew, and on October 31, 1517, Halloween annoyed them yet again. Martin Luther, who was a Catholic monk, picked that day to nail a list of his grievances with the church to the door of Wittenberg Chapel in Germany. This caused the beginning of the religious upheaval known as the Protestant Reformation. Luther knew that many people would show up the next day, All Saints' Day, to venerate the enormous collection of relics and bones of the saints at the chapel and see his post made on Halloween night.

As the Reformation brought a clash between the Catholics and the new Protestants, the observances of All Saints' Day and All Souls' Day diminished somewhat since Protestants did not believe in the saints. What happened to the folkloric celebration of Halloween, you might ask? The traditions were still carried on in some households, and less than one hundred years later some of the practices gained popularity yet again, finding a new home on November 5.

Guy Fawkes

On November 5, 1605, the drama over the Protestant Reformation came to a head when Guy Fawkes was arrested while guarding a large cache of explosives that he and his group of fellow conspirators had planned to use to blow up the British Parliament and assassinate King James I. Yes, *that* Guy Fawkes—the one whose mask we see worn in *V for Vendetta* and the face representing the modern network of hacktivists called Anonymous, that's Guy Fawkes from 1605. The plot to blow up Parliament now foiled, Fawkes was tortured and executed.

The king had survived the plot, and the celebration of Gunpowder Treason Day, also known as Bonfire Night and later called Guy Fawkes Night, sprang up immediately on November 5. Effigies of Guy Fawkes were burned on bonfires. This wasn't originally the fun celebration it is today but an often angry and sometimes violent event. Gangs of young men in Guy Fawkes disguises (known as "Guys") roamed, committing acts of vandalism and rolling burning barrels through the streets. In late October leading up to Guy Fawkes Night, kids would now go door to door asking for firewood for the bonfire and money—"A penny for the Guy." The celebration had enveloped the traditions of bonfires, begging, and pranks.

A New World

This was shortly before the time when the Puritans were heading for America. They wanted nothing to do with Halloween as they settled in the new world, recognizing Halloween's Pagan roots and the Catholic co-opting of the holiday. Many of them settled in Massachusetts and held contempt for anything to do with the occult; this fearful obsession eventually led to the tragedy of the Salem Witch Trials ravaging their community and costing twenty people their lives.

Not all the American colonies were so fearful of the spirit world and witchcraft, though; the celebration of Halloween grew to popularity in Virginia and other southern colonies. These areas had larger Catholic, Episcopalian, and Anglican colonists at the time who brought with them the traditions of Halloween. Lavish and fun "play parties" were held on Halloween night that included feasts; tales of ghosts, magic, and the supernatural; and even divination games, which were mostly used to discover the romantic futures of the young adults in attendance.

By the 1840s the potato famine brought in a larger influx of Irish immigrants, and as they joined the American communities they shared the rich Halloween customs. Halloween became even more popular in the United States. The Irish tradition of carving jack-o'-lanterns out of turnips was soon adapted to the easier-to-carve American pumpkins, and the classic Halloween icon was born. Along with the more magical aspects of Halloween, the traditions of playing tricks and pranks came to America as well.

Mischief Managed

By the early twentieth century Halloween had become a night of mostly mischief in America and Canada. Pulling pranks was the main Halloween activity back then, and we're not just talking about smashing pumpkins or toilet papering the trees; these kids were pulling big pranks like removing gates from their hinges, tipping over outhouses, or putting large items on people's roofs or haystacks.

Halloween vandalism soon increased, possibly due to the pressure of society at the time during the Great

Depression. Halloween was becoming dangerous and costly. Reckless activities like derailing streetcars, releasing livestock into the streets, smashing windows, and setting fires was becoming more commonplace. Gate Night, Mischief Night, and Hell Night were all names being used for Halloween.

Finally, neighborhoods and local businesses decided that something must be done. To curb unruly activities, many cities began holding Halloween parades with treats and prizes for kids who attended in their costumes. Among the first cities to take this approach were Anoka, MN; Allentown, PA; Hiawatha, KS; and Chicago, IL.

Big Halloween parties that included costume contests, games, bonfires, and of course treats for the kids were hosted by schools and communities. Radio stations would plan giveaways to be announced on the radio after the parties so kids would race home and listen to see if they had won instead of running amuck in the streets.

Halloween party guides known as *Dennison's Bogie Books* were popular guides of the time and inspired homemakers to host their own Halloween parties. They started opening up their doors to local costumed children and

TIP 1
Vintage Halloween Bogie Books

Original copies of *Dennison's Bogie Books*, which are Halloween entertainment guides from the early twentieth century, are pretty expensive if you can find one. The good news is that reproductions of those books have been published so that anyone can have one. With cool old-fashioned Halloween ideas and great vintage illustrations, they're really fun books.

passing out treats; in some communities children shared clever songs or a joke at the door as well. Premade crepe paper costumes and paper masks were sold, but many people opted for homemade. I find photos of people in their homemade costumes from this era delightfully creepy!

By the late 1930s kids were giving up most of the pranking and vandalism and joining in the fun of Halloween festivities offered instead. The term "trick-or-treat" had spread from Canada in the 1920s through some areas in America, and by the late '30s it was beginning to be used as an agreement between homeowners and would-be vandals as a trade of sorts for protection from pranks.

Tricks and Treats

The sugar rationing during WWII and hard times in general during that time slowed the celebration of Halloween, when many festivities had to be cancelled. But after the war and the end of rationing, Halloween parties and going door to door came back more popular than ever. Treats at parties and the early days of trick-or-treating included homemade popcorn balls, cookies, apples, and some candies, but you were just as likely to get nuts or coins as loose candy corn. Some residents weren't fans of the practice of trick-or-treating and would drop a rock into unsuspecting trick-or-treaters' bags. Soon the baby boomers were born, and trick-or-treating spread like crazy. The traditions of door to door begging and disguises were reborn and now cemented in American culture as modern-day trick-or-treat.

In the early 1950s some clever candy companies started advertising their products as great treats for neighborhood kids. We also saw the first mini candy bars on the market, possibly as a suggestion for trick-or-treaters. Cereal companies produced mini packages of sugary cereal to offer as treats.

While many kids wore homemade costumes, the first plastic storebought costumes became available: characters from television shows were popular, such as Casper the Friendly Ghost, Zorro, or Howdy Doody, and the ever-popular witch. Many of these boxed costumes boasted that they were flame retardant and had large eye holes for safety, which were improvements on the flammable paper designs of the past. Many people let their

Halloween TV specials were soon to become a new tradition—a modern version of ghost stories.

kids out on their own to trick-or-treat back then, trusting in their neighbors and the world they lived in. In 1966 the animated special *It's the Great Pumpkin, Charlie Brown* aired for the first time, and Halloween TV specials were soon to become a new tradition—a modern version of ghost stories.

By the '60s and '70s Halloween was quite mainstream, and my friends and I were riding the wave of Halloween bounty prepared by the generations of revelers that had came before us. Neighbors filled pillowcases and plastic pumpkins with prepackaged candy that was now being mass-produced just for the occasion. Both in plastic

storebought costumes and homemade creations, young-
sters took to the streets and ended up with armloads of
wrapped candy. Occasionally trick-or-treaters did still
get homemade treats, such as popcorn balls, and even
some coins.

By the '70s most houses in many neighborhoods
were participating in trick-or-treating. Hinged paper
cut-out decorations in the windows and carved pumpkins greeted the hoards of kids collecting their spoils. It
never occurred to any of the kids that they had anything
to worry about, but soon parents announced that they
would be inspecting the piles of loot before kids could
eat the first piece.

There were stories of people tampering with treats,
reports of razor blades in apples, and poison or drugs in
candy. Parents were scared for their kids, and some of
the community trust that people felt on Halloween had
been tarnished. In these cases, most people heard the initial reports but had not heard the outcomes of these stories, when it was later discovered that the cases reported
were perpetrated by the trick-or-treaters' own families
or that other reports of tampering were urban legends

and myths unfounded in fact. The damage had been done: people were afraid on Halloween, but less of the supernatural than of their own neighbors, which flies in the face of Halloween's community spirit.

The scares about treats meant parents often checked candy, tossing anything that was unwrapped or that looked suspicious. People still gave out apples and homemade treats, but parents inspected apples to make sure the skin hadn't been broken, and I recall that many parents cut up any Halloween apples for kids.

I vividly remember being a teenager in October 1982 and having baked and decorated some really cool cookies to pass out for Halloween when the tragic news reports came in that there were people who had been poisoned by Tylenol that had been tampered with. We immediately stamped our address on the bags for the cookies as a last-ditch effort in hopes that people wouldn't toss them, but that year we hardly had any trick-or-treaters. People feared tampering of anything on the store shelves, so random people passing out treats seemed even more suspect. We never saw homemade treats being passed out after that year, only completely sealed commercial treats, although trick-or-treating did make a rebound yet again.

Even with the scares, Halloween and trick-or-treat never lost its magic through the 1970s and '80s. Another development that started in the early '70s and finally tapered down in the '90s was the resurgence of some major vandalism, especially in Detroit, where there was no amount of candy to assuage the vandals setting fires there—not just a few fires, hundreds of arson fires were set over the days surrounding Halloween, especially on October 30, to the point where people in those areas began using the name Devil's Night or Mischief Night for the night before Halloween. When the Devil's Night fires reached their pinnacle in 1994, city officials and residents banded together and patrolled neighborhoods; the number of fires dropped dramatically.

Modern Halloween Celebrations

A wonderful and important tradition that got traction in the 1980s and '90s and is still continued today are the celebrations of Halloween by the LGBTQ community. The first unofficial "street party" style celebration for this community was in the '70s in San Francisco's Castro district. By the '80s Greenwich Village, Key West, and West Hollywood were getting into the act.

Halloween became a time for the members of this often marginalized community to let their flags fly and express themselves—or even larger-than-life versions of themselves—to help offset the oppression felt throughout the rest of the year. For many people, Halloween became an empowering night of freedom because of these events. Some of the best Halloween parades are held by the LGBTQ communities; everyone is welcome to join in the festivities as long as they're respectful of their fellow celebrants.

Today Halloween is big business and big fun too. The Halloween costumes and decorations that once took up one shelf in the general store now have several aisles in big-box stores, and entire pop-up stores appear in towns all over the United States. Animatronics that scream, move, and light up have replaced the crepe paper skeletons of yesteryear. The kids of the '60s and '70s loved Halloween so much that they never gave it up, and they never stopped celebrating it even when they became adults. Many adults now dress up to trick-or-treat with their kids. People spend many hours and tons of money every year on decorations for their yards and homes, both for their own satisfaction and to impress the trick-or-treaters in their neighborhoods.

Adult costume sales are bigger than ever, and some of those costumes are smaller than ever. Costume parties at bars and music clubs are heavily attended. Sexy costumes have become more popular, but we've also seen more creative costumes than ever before. Many people who grew up enchanted with the idea of trying on a new persona on Halloween have gone on to enjoy costuming in the form of cosplay events like comic book, science fiction, horror, and steampunk conventions.

In many ways, modern Halloween celebrations give us the opportunity to look at death in a more lighthearted way and even laugh at it. As cathartic and fun experiences to test our bravery, professional haunted houses have become popular events all across the country. Día de los Muertos—another ancient festival of the dead that was grafted onto All Saints' Day and All Souls' Day— has found its way joyously from the streets of Mexico and South America to many festivals in the United States.

Postcards from Halloween's Past

One of the most interesting and beautiful ways to get a glimpse into Halloween history is through vintage Halloween postcards. The really old ones are in public domain, and you can find lots of them on the internet. Vintage postcards are a fascinating glimpse into the trends, fashions, and customs of the times. These postcards also make great décor items for your home. I've added some of these images to big jar candles with a glue stick, adding glowing vintage Halloween charm to my tables and bookshelves.

This festival teaches us not to fear death but to honor our beloved dead with happiness for the lives they lived. Of course, Día de los Muertos is not Halloween, but we are now seeing party goods with the classic sugar skull motifs on the shelves right next to the Halloween paraphernalia. American Halloween is a melting pot of traditions carried over from the proud lines of immigrants from far and wide who make up the country.

Rediscovering Samhain

The revival of Pagan faiths in the UK and the US in the early twentieth century means that many people who grew up with the secular celebration of Halloween still celebrate it with delight but have also rediscovered Samhain, the spiritual root of this fun modern celebration. Modern Pagans, witches, Druids, and Wiccans often recognize Samhain as being separate but parallel to Halloween. These groups attempt to bring the ancient practices of Samhain and the rest of the old celebrations of the Wheel of the Year into modern times.

There are some people who prefer to judge harshly those of different faiths, cultures, or orientations, as if the existence of other kinds of people threatens their own truths. Acting out of fear instead of understanding only shuts down human progress instead of enhancing it. Halloween has grown into a celebration that brings us together. We celebrate in costumes and can become anyone; in a way, it equalizes us all. It makes us recognize the masks that we wear every day—and hopefully we realize that beneath those masks we aren't that different after all. Can we humans of differing backgrounds find common ground in the joy of Halloween?

This celebration has come full circle. From its mystical origins it has changed and morphed through the ages, as we all have. The celebration picked up practices from other sources and continues to do so. It's important to know where we come from, for in that we can better see where we are and where we are going. This holds true for our customs and practices as well because those practices are part of who we are. Blazing ahead for future generations, Halloween has carried its energies through the centuries from deep memory. The rituals may have changed over the years, but the traces of its roots have remained.

CREATING A
HAUNTING
ATMOSPHERE

Every October our houses become transformed into magical places—haunted houses, if you will. Whimsical pumpkins welcome visitors with Halloween curb appeal, skeletons dance from the rafters, tiny effigies of ghosts and witches in their pointy hats find their homes on bookshelves. Bundles of corn stalks seem to sprout from our porches, we break out those cauldron coffee mugs, and sometimes even headstones—representing our awareness of mortality—take up residence on the front lawn. How many of you are humming that cheerful tune "This Is Halloween" from the 1993 film *The Nightmare Before Christmas* as you delightedly open the boxes and totes that have been hiding away in the underworld of your basement, attic, or garage for a year? Do you dust away the real cobwebs so that you can put up fake ones? I do.

Decorating for Halloween both inside and out has become a huge undertaking in many households today, and it marks the beginning of the season of magic. Some people spend a small fortune on their Halloween décor, while others craft clever DIY creations; many of us have a mix of both. Most witches I know like to add magical elements to their Halloween/Samhain décor as well, enchanting candles and using color magic or other forms of magical symbolism.

There are many different styles: some houses glitter with mystical scenes that are whimsical and fun while others run the spectrum from creepy to downright gruesome and terrifying. There's no right or wrong way to do it; it all depends on your style. Halloween is the time of the year when we get to step outside of ourselves—and not just with costumes but with our personal spaces. At any other time of the year the neighbors might call the police if they saw a femur in your yard, but in October it's all in good fun!

Do you dust away the real cobwebs so that you can put up fake ones? I do.

TIP 3
Halloween on a Shoestring

Early on November 1, run by the Halloween aisles at local big-box stores or get over to that Halloween pop-up store before it pops back down again. Most Halloween décor, costumes, and servingware will be on clearance at deep discounts. Every year after Halloween I stock up on fancy Halloween paper plates and napkins, plus I usually add several décor items, candles, and more to my Halloween totes before I put everything away. It's a golden opportunity to get a nice stash of discounted loot for next year's Halloween. Make sure you get there early or I'll beat you to all the good bargains!

Halloween Décor Themes

Here are some Halloween décor theme ideas that you might enjoy; you can also make them all magically enchanted. They are just jumping-off places, really; as you read them, note if one speaks to you; you can use any of these suggestions and adjust according to your personal taste and resources. Take these snippets of inspiration and let your creativity and magical inspiration run wild!

Vintage

One of the more popular styles in recent times is a throwback to vintage designs from the 1940s through the '60s. This style reflects the time when the holiday we celebrate today was pretty much becoming cemented into modern culture. There are many online printables and lots that you can make yourself, too. This cool throwback to the old days can be achieved with papier-mâché, vintage postcards, orange-and-black paper banners, crepe paper streamers, paper lanterns, tissue-paper honeycomb decorations, and cartoony cats, pumpkins, and ghosts.

For many witches, looking back in time helps us connect with our spiritual ancestors. Sprinkle rosemary about or add rosemary oil to your jack-o'-lantern candles to represent remembrance and help you connect to the spirits of witches from days gone by.

Gothic

This is the Halloween décor for your dark heart, as this theme reflects the remembrance of ancestors and the recognition of mortality. Lots of people love a dark, scary party for Halloween. Black lace tablecloths and black cheesecloth draped on the windows add to the creepy vibe, as do candles in every corner. Skulls and bones are perfect for this theme, along with black roses, ravens, spiderwebs, and rats scattered about.

Basically, think Dracula's castle: headstones fit right in inside, outside, or both. Apothecary jars, bottles, and specimen jars can display candy or little horrors. You can also print out anatomical illustrations and pop them into thrifted frames. An ancestor altar with photos of your beloved dead fits perfectly into this theme, tying in a serious and reverent magical purpose to a fun design aesthetic.

Autumn Harvest

When decorating with a harvest theme, pumpkins and bales of straw are the stars of the show as you celebrate the magic of abundance. A scarecrow is perfect for welcoming guests. Corn stalks on the front porch reflect a harvest motif. Agricultural-themed fall decorations look great with a harvest theme: jar candles tied with burlap ribbon, mini pumpkins and gourds scattered about, and autumn leaf garlands reflect the season. You can draw equal-armed crosses using cinnamon oil to enchant the elements of your décor, bringing abundance into your home and life.

Movie Theme

Why not use one of your favorite Halloween or horror films for your inspiration when decorating? This is a theme that celebrates fantasy and stepping inside another world. Choose your favorite film, determine its color scheme and visual esthetic, and apply it to your décor. For *Practical Magic*, use bottles of herbs, a giant decorative book, maybe a bowl of frogs, and brooms in every corner. For *The Nightmare Before Christmas,* use lots of black and white and add a Halloween-themed Christmas tree. For

TIP 4
Silent Horrors

If you're having a big Halloween party and you're not planning on screening a movie to watch, you might just want to employ that big blank TV in your living room to add more spooky ambiance to your space. You can't beat the extremely creepy factor of black-and-white silent horror films; these often come with background music, so just turn the sound down on the television and play your own music. Some wicked cool choices for haunting your TV on Halloween night include *Nosferatu*, *Faust*, *The Fall of the House of Usher*, and *The Cabinet of Doctor Caligari*.

an Alfred Hitchcock Halloween tribute, decorate with tons of birds and make sure there's a bloody shower curtain in the bathroom.

Anyway, you get the idea; what's your favorite movie? Watch it while you take notes for ideas to include in your Halloween décor. Other ideas for movie-themed décor include printing out movie quotes and glueing them onto jar candles scattered about the room. Framed movie stills and posters can add to the theme. Also consider carving a movie-themed jack-o'-lantern. Don't forget to serve popcorn, the traditional movie treat. Magically, popcorn brings good luck and abundance; it is said that financial or romantic goals spoken over popping popcorn will manifest. I think it's worth a try!

Ghosts Are Afoot

Shades of white and gray add ambiance to your house on Halloween and recognize the aspect of spirits on this night. Classic jack-o'-lanterns are associated with spiritual presences; if you're doing a ghostly theme, you can use classic orange pumpkins, white pumpkins, turnips, or a mix. Your ghosts can be represented as terrifying or ethereal, depending on what you prefer. Skulls and skeletons work well for a ghost theme. You can purchase ghost figures, but making them isn't hard. Using items like cheesecloth, plastic wrap, and box tape, I've used a white Styrofoam wig head and chiffon robe with great effect. Add white spider webs all around and drape furniture in white sheets to mimic an abandoned haunted house. Hang creepy old-time photos of people in Halloween costumes in thrifted frames around the house.

This is a theme that truly reminds us of the thin veil between the worlds. Burn sweetgrass to welcome helpful spirits. Add frankincense, sandalwood, or angelica oil to your candles to raise the vibrations of your space and welcome in only benevolent spirits.

Magical Cottage

Yeah, you knew I couldn't pass this one by. I have little kitchen witch figures that I keep in my kitchen all year long; I add to their numbers every Halloween. A witch's cottage theme can be fun: pumpkins, bats, and standard Halloween fare get a magical makeover with witchy additions. Hang multiple witch hats from the ceiling with fishing line and tacks so that they appear to be floating; they also look cool in the trees outside. Create a witch's parking lot with a sign and several decorated brooms. Make book covers for several large books out of paper grocery bags and decorate them like spell books displayed in a big stack.

Potion bottles set around the rooms make a magical statement. Hang up a rustic branch on the wall, with several bundles of herbs tied with orange-and-black Halloween ribbon dangling from the branch along with paper moons and stars. Witch's familiars like black cats, crows, bats, owls, and even frogs can be placed strategically about to add life to the space.

*Create a witch's
parking lot with a sign
and several decorated brooms.*

In the tradition of the wise, witchy healers of old, you can burn a couple bay leaves in your witch's cottage to raise positive vibrations, banish fear, and boost mental sharpness.

Symbols of Halloween

As we think about breaking out our Halloween decorations, no matter the style we prefer, some of our special seasonal knickknacks have things in common. As we peruse the retail stores, dig through the latest Halloween editions of magazines, and search Pinterest boards for ideas, we become aware that there are many classic symbols associated with Halloween.

Did you ever wonder what the iconic symbols of Halloween mean and how they came to be associated with the holiday to begin with? One might think that they're just part of Halloween because we consider them scary, and that may be true of some modern trends such as hockey masks, political figures, or creepy clowns. The classic, age-old symbology of Halloween, however, has roots in older times, many going all the way back to Samhain, and all can be considered magical symbols to add to your Halloween/Samhain magic.

Once you know the story behind each symbol, it will mean more when you see them in décor and on cards, treats, and costumes. Here's my "witch's dozen" (that's thirteen) classic symbols of Halloween and where they come from.

Ghosts

Ghosts and spirits are one of the foundations of Halloween; after all, it's the time of the year when the veil between the physical world and the otherworld is at its thinnest. According to folklore that goes all the way back to Samhain, ghosts of the deceased and the more elemental spirits of the land may be roaming this time of year. When Samhain became Halloween, many pranksters would dress as ghosts and then blame their shenanigans on spirits, thus keeping the idea of supernatural beings very much in the forefront of the holiday.

We see both scary and fun ghosts in décor everywhere on Halloween. Even humorous or simple-looking renditions of ghosts that we see hearken back to the idea that at Halloween the spirits walk with us. Use ghost figures in magic to communicate with other realms or rid yourself of old habits.

Skeletons

Skeletons and skulls aren't just morbid Goth decorations; they remind us that we're mortal. Bones are all that is left in the physical world once our spirit has moved on and time has passed by; the skeletons remind us of our ancestors. Since Samhain was a celebration of the ancestors, skeletons and skulls are a perfect symbol of the season to remind us of our own mortality and the generations whose history runs through our veins.

The symbolism of the Mexican festival Día de los Muertos, celebrated from October 31 through November 2, has recently become entwined in Halloween culture as well; the festive decorated skulls and skeletons are also symbols of their beloved dead. Skulls and skeletons can be included in magic to connect with ancestors and remind us of our life's purpose and mortality.

Bats

Bats have been a longtime symbol of Halloween, and it's not because they're scary; I've met a few, and they're really not. We have many caves in our area, and we cherish our bat population. Bats were noticed visiting the Samhain bonfires; as the revelers danced and feasted, the bats feasted too—on bugs! Flying insects were drawn to the light of the fire, creating a feast for these winged mammals. In October bats are building up their fat reserves so that they can hibernate over the winter; Samhain and Halloween bonfires would have been golden opportunities to get the last of the bugs before their winter's sleep. Much like the ancient Celts, bats were feasting and preparing. Bat symbols can be used in magic for big life changes, courage, and seeing the unseen.

Witches

Witches have been seen as caricatures associated with Halloween for years, but the real witch is a human being that honors the earth and honors the old ways with powerful prayers referred to as magic spells. Witches commune with nature and work magic with the cycles of the seasons. When the churches converted the Celts, they called their old traditions of magic and reverence for the earth evil. In the Middle Ages they even portrayed witches in art wearing pointed hats, which was the style worn by country women in the last areas to give up Samhain traditions.

Since the 1800s, witches flying on brooms with black cats have been a fun staple of Halloween cards. Real witches and the folklore traditions associated with Samhain and Halloween, however, have been looked at as either wise yet mysterious figures or demonized through the ages, just as Halloween also has ebbed and flowed throughout history but never died out completely. Witch figures can be included in spells to embrace your personal power or free your spirit from societal expectations.

Black Cats

Black cats are associated with witches and seen in images riding with a witch on a broom with arched back and hair standing on end, but is the cat as a witch's familiar the only Halloween association? There actually are legends of a creature known as a *cait sidhe* (roughly pronounced *ket-she*) among the Irish and in the Scottish Highlands. This phantom is a large supernatural black cat with a white spot on its chest. Some legends say it is a faery or witch in cat form and can transform only nine times, hence the cat's nine lives. And if you leave a bowl of milk out for the cait sidhe on Samhain night, your home will be blessed.

Black cat candles are used to magically turn your luck around, especially in gambling and finances.

Owls

Owls are another nocturnal animal, like the bat, but they are also portrayed on antique greeting cards being chummy with both witches and black cats. Owls were sometimes suggested to be witches in disguise, but it is also suggested that they may have joined the bats in airborne harvest feasts, snatching up large moths or even small bats themselves from the air above the Samhain bonfires.

Owls are also often associated with wisdom; many dark goddesses who rule over the dark half of the year have owls as their sacred animals. Include owl symbols in your spellwork to guide you through dark times, find wisdom, and seek the truth.

Cauldrons

Cauldrons on Halloween are often portrayed as being filled with some kind of magical brew or even poison, but to the Celts it was associated with the Goddess, rebirth, and abundance. In Pagan folklore the womb of the Goddess is a great cauldron where souls would enter after death, waiting to be reborn—a perfect symbol for a festival of the dead. It's also a symbol of the Celtic god known as the Dagda, whose cauldron was magically always full of abundance. Halloween hearkens back to ancient Samhain feasts, and the cauldron is an actual cooking pot that was used as a symbol of plenty by the Celts and many other cultures as well. When putting together your Halloween feast, consider how that slow cooker or pressure cooker full of chili is nothing more than a modern cauldron transforming your harvest from the grocery store into a nourishing autumn feast for all. A cauldron can be used for many purposes in magical work, including manifesting goals, transformation, and abundance.

Scarecrows

Scarecrows, believe it or not, go all the way back to ancient Egypt. Many cultures have used scarecrows to protect their fields from birds, and they were considered symbols of good fortune. From the anatomically correct Greek scarecrows meant to represent the god Priapus to Japanese armed scarecrows or the German scarecrows that look like witches, it's a farmer's companion that crosses cultures. Because it protects the grain in the fields, scarecrows are an old symbol of the harvest and prosperity. A scarecrow is also an iconic effigy figure. Representing the spirit of the land and the harvest itself, it is sometimes burned after harvest festivals and the ashes returned to the earth that it guarded. Sometimes humorous, sometimes terrifying, this is another character that we've seen represented on vintage Halloween postcards for ages associated with the harvest and death aspect of Halloween. A scarecrow figure can be used in a spell as a poppet for sending healing energy, and it can also be enchanted as a magical guardian.

Ravens and Crows

Ravens and crows come from a family of birds called corvids, and both are associated with Halloween. Crows and ravens were seen on the battlefield and in the grain fields, associating them with both death and the harvest, prevalent themes of Samhain and Halloween. Corvids picked the ground after the grain harvest was brought in, looking for spilled grain, and they also dug for bugs in the ground. Corvids were yet another animal that people suspected were either witches or faeries in disguise, probably because of their odd behavior compared to other animals. Corvids are especially intelligent; some use rudimentary tools, figure out puzzles, and like to collect shiny objects, so you can see why people might find them unnervingly intelligent animals and possibly supernatural. Include images of ravens or crows in luck and protection spells or to connect with the magical realms.

Jack-o'-Lanterns

Jack-o'-lanterns were a tradition in Ireland and spread to the Celtic regions. They were originally carved from turnips until the Irish immigrated to America and discovered that pumpkins grown there were larger and easier to carve. The tradition caught on in America, and soon everyone was carving jack-o'-lanterns.

There are many versions of the jack-o'-lantern origin story; all revolve around a man named Jack. Jack was a stingy blacksmith who was always playing mean tricks, eventually tricking the devil himself. When Jack died, he couldn't get into heaven, and hell wouldn't have him, so he carved out a turnip to hold the coal the devil gave him as a consolation prize and roamed the earth with it. People have been using jack-o'-lanterns to protect themselves from spirits and to frighten others on Halloween

Pumpkin Seeds

Don't toss those pumpkin seeds when you carve up those jack-o'-lanterns! Pumpkin seeds are associated with magic for granting wishes, prosperity, and protection. Roast them for a delicious crunchy, magical Halloween treat.

Separate the seeds as best you can; putting them in a bowl of water can help you separate the seeds from the rest of the pulp since pumpkin seeds float. Rinse them in a colander, add them to a pot of boiling saltwater for 10 minutes, then drain. Dry the seeds on paper towels. Put them on a rimmed cookie sheet and drizzle with a bit of olive oil and a couple teaspoons of salt and toss well. I like to sprinkle mine with sea salt, but you can use your choice of seasonings, then bake at 325 degrees Fahrenheit for about 20 minutes or until crispy.

ever since. For many people, the jack-o'-lantern is the last remnant of the Samhain bonfires—a carved pumpkin carrying on the flame from this old festival. Magical uses for pumpkins and jack-o'-lanterns include protection, abundance, and wishing.

Spiders

Spiders and Halloween seem to go hand in hand today, but where did the connection come from? The connection with spiders and Halloween may be attributed to the fact that they would have been seen in the crypts and mausoleums used to house the dead from ancient Roman times onward. To determine the meaning of spiders as an iconic presence at Halloween, look to the web that they weave. The web of a spider has come to represent time as well as fate, both themes relevant during the time of the dying land and the onset of winter.

There is a superstition that if you see a spider on Halloween, it may be one of your ancestors checking up on you. There are many superstitions that killing a spider is bad luck; I always catch and release whenever I can. Use the symbol of a spider for communication magic; the spider is a great totem for creative people and can also magically connect you to the universe helping you speak your truth and be heard. Spiders can also be a symbol of increased finances.

Masks

Masks and costumes go back to the very roots of Halloween. The Celts would dress in strange clothing and wear either masks or face paint when they were out on Samhain to hide in plain sight from the wandering spirits, ghosts, and faeries roaming about during the time when the veil between our world and theirs was the thinnest. The tradition carried on when Christianity took over the holiday and dubbed it All Souls' Day and people went guising or performed mumming processions in costume.

Costuming is rooted in ancient ceremonial practices across cultures. It seems to be something that can give us a great feeling of power and awaken our creative minds. Wearing masks on Halloween can either give license to create mischief or be a transformation tool as the wearer embodies a new persona for the night. Wear a mask for magic relating to transformation or empowering inner aspects of your personality.

Orange and Black

Orange and black, as we all know, are the official colors of Halloween. While the choice of these high-contrast colors may seem like a marketing choice, have you ever wondered about their magical significance? Witches know black is a color that neutralizes outside energies; it's a color used in many spiritual practices for psychic protection and divination. Halloween falls well into the dark half of the year, so black is a perfect representation of this holiday.

Orange is a harvest color, representing the changing leaves. On a metaphysical level, orange is also a color that breaks down barriers; since Halloween's deepest roots are tied to the concept of the barrier between the physical and spirit worlds being thin and opening, this makes a lot of sense. Orange brings joy and inspires strength to face our fears.

On the deepest level, think of the colors you would see around an ancient Samhain bonfire: the orange of the fire set against the black of night. They didn't have pumpkins, candy corn, or black-and-orange streamers, but the color palette was there in the celebration from the start.

The color black is used in many spiritual practices for psychic protection and divination.

• • • •

Now that we know the symbols of Halloween are much more than they appear on the surface, it makes us mindful of what they mean when we add them to our homes. Symbols are an important part of our psyche, human culture, and magic, allowing us to connect with the bigger picture. It's also fun to have interesting knowledge to share with others about our favorite time of the year. Knowing the root of what symbols mean makes them even more meaningful when I use them to create an atmosphere or spellwork in my home during Halloween.

• EXERCISE 1 •
Pumpkin Carving 101

I bet most people reading this have carved a pumpkin before, but I'm going to share some tried and true tips for making a really cool jack-o'-lantern.

- Choose a perfect pumpkin: firm and with no soft spots, nicks, or gouges taken out of it.
- Make sure the stem is attached; a 3–5-inch stem will help your pumpkin last longer, while a loose or missing stem will make your pumpkin rot faster.
- Never carry the pumpkin by the stem; instead, carry it from the bottom.
- Set it on a flat surface to make sure that its bottom is flat and not wobbly.

Tools

Gather your tools and cover your workspace with newspaper or plastic. Serrated knives work well; I've often used a thin steak knife. One of those pumpkin carving kits, especially if you're worried about cutting yourself, works just fine—those tools are great for carving through pumpkin flesh, and it's hard to cut yourself with one. Wash the outside of the pumpkin and cut the top off around the stem. Make the hole at least big enough to get your hand in, and angle the knife handle away from the stem so that the top doesn't fall in.

Scrape the inside of the pumpkin as clean as you can because all those stringy pumpkin guts will actually make it rot faster—who knew? The old standard method is to scrape the inside out with a big metal spoon. Now they make attachments for your drill to help clean out the inside of pumpkins, and if you follow the instructions, they work well. You can also attach a beater from an electric mixer into the drill chuck.

Whether you're using a beater or a pumpkin-gutting attachment, the procedure is the same. First, put your drill on high speed, which makes all the difference. Now, I know you want to plunge it into the bottom of the pumpkin and turn it on, but resist the urge. Instead, start high up on the inside of the pumpkin, working around the top edge. Next, work a bit lower, circling the pumpkin's opening below the area you already did. Dump some of the guts out and continue circling your way down the edges. You'll do the bottom last. Keep dumping as you go. If the strings get wrapped around the tool, remove the tool from the drill and slide the glob of strings right off the back, then replace the tool. Using a drill tool won't hurt your seeds either, so you can save them for roasting or planting later.

Carving from a Template

Once your pumpkin is empty, you're ready to carve either freehand or with a template. Many kits come with templates, or you can find free templates online. If you want to make your own, it's not hard to do. I use a piece of computer paper to sketch out my pattern. Keep in mind that you can't make bits of pumpkin float in the middle of a carved-out section (if you find a spell to do that, let me know), so you'll want to plan your design with that in mind; much like a stencil for spray-painting, everything needs to stay attached to the rest of the pumpkin. While you're thinking about designs, consider adding magical symbols, sigils, or runes to your design to boost the jack-o'-lantern's protective energies; it is a magical protection talisman, after all.

It's easier than you think to carve from a photograph. There are lots of photo-editing programs these days. I use Photoshop or Photoshop Elements, or try free editing software like PicMonkey, Gimp, or a phone app with color and contrast editing abilities. Whichever software you use, convert it to black and white first, then bring up the contrast and dial the brightness up and down until it looks good.

If this all seems too complex, try doing an internet search for "posterize a photo free." There are several sites where you can just upload your photo, choose two or three levels of color, and it will do it for you. I also found websites using a search for "put your face on a pumpkin" that convert any high-contrast photo to look like it's actually on a pumpkin. You can print it out on 8½ x 11 paper and use that as your template; easy, right? For portraits, I like to use the "next level" method described below for both peeling and cutting through the pumpkin.

To transfer your template onto your pumpkin, begin by putting notches in the edges of the template, cutting from the edge toward the center about an inch or so in. Don't cut into the design—this helps it wrap around the pumpkin better. Secure the template with masking tape, making sure it's secure and won't slide around. Using a nail or thumbtack, punch small holes all along the lines of the template into the pumpkin. Make these holes close together, about $\frac{1}{16}$ of an inch, or 2 mm.

Once you've transferred the design, remove the paper. Look at the template for a guide, and use a red permanent marker to connect the dots and trace out your design. I use red instead of black because it's easier to remove when your pumpkin is done. If it's a highly detailed design, it helps to color in the parts that you want to carve away with the red marker, leaving the parts that will stay orange. Start from the center and work on the small detail areas first; this way you don't put pressure on the larger areas and weaken them as you work. Once you're done, hairspray will remove any marker.

Taking It to the Next Level

"Next level" jack-o'-lanterns aren't as difficult as you might think. If you can color in a coloring book, you have the skills to do more advanced jack-o'-lanterns. A great way to amp up your jack-o'-lanterns is by using a peeling technique. Peeling the skin in some areas and cutting all the way through in others gives you more dimension and shading; it also works great for designs with lots of details.

Just remember the shading works like this: the darkest is the orange pumpkin peel, the middle shade is the peeled flesh, and the lightest shade is cutting all the way through. The trick to peeling the skin is to first cut around the lines about ¼-inch deep with a craft knife such as an X-Acto; then you can use a chisel, linoleum-carving tools, or even the tip of a butter knife to remove the dark orange skin, exposing the yellow flesh beneath. Make sure that you scrape the inside of the pumpkin thinner than usual to help more light shine through. Light it with an electric pumpkin light as you go so that you can see how it's looking. It will look weird until you light it up.

• EXERCISE 2 •

How to Make Your
Jack-o'-Lanterns Last Longer

I love carving intricate pumpkins. I've done business logos and even won a pumpkin-carving contest once with a portrait of Eric Draven from *The Crow*. Usually I am so darned busy the day before Halloween that instead of amazing creations, I end up rushing through some pretty standard jack-o'-lantern faces just to have them done and out before they rot. However, I've done some research and discovered ways to make jack-o'-lanterns last longer, so now I can put more time into my jack-o'-lanterns the week before, and I know they'll make it to Halloween.

• • • •

PLEASE NOTE: If you plan to cook and eat your pumpkins after Halloween or serve food out of them, do not use any of these preservation techniques; just carve them on Halloween. Kitchen witches know that pumpkin is a food that provides health benefits as well as magical protection, prosperity, and wishing magic. Cooking up a fresh Halloween jack-o'-lantern carved the night before adds extra energy to an already powerful magical food.

The biggest enemies to a carved pumpkin are mold and dehydration. Whether it's carved or not, never display your pumpkin on concrete, which sucks moisture out of your pumpkin, making it decompose faster. Set your pumpkin on a board or a square of cardboard. After carving your pumpkin, spritz it inside and out with a mixture of bleach and water. Add 4 tablespoons of bleach to a 16-ounce bottle and fill the rest with water. Spray the entire pumpkin with this formula once a day, inside and out and especially the cuts. Wear only clothes that you don't care about getting bleach on, and do it outside, away from anything that might get damaged by bleach. Bleach water is the best way to make your jack-o'-lantern last a long time, as it rehydrates the pumpkin and kills off mold and mildew. The pumpkin still will eventually rot, but—depending on your climate and other factors— your pumpkin can last up to ten days. If it starts to look like it's drying out, dunk it in a bucket of water, add 1 tablespoon of bleach per gallon of water, and let it soak for a couple hours. Your pumpkin will bounce right back!

Not everyone wants to use bleach, and I totally get it; it's a harsh chemical. If you live where squirrels might nibble at your pumpkins, then you might not want to use bleach, although my squirrels wouldn't touch them when I used it. For a more natural pumpkin spritz, try adding 1 tablespoon of borax and 13 drops of lavender oil to your 16-ounce spray bottle and shake before you spray. Lavender oil has antifungal properties and offers protection magic, so as a witchy bonus this one will actually help enchant your jack-o'-lanterns to ward off bad vibes and dark spirits. If you don't want to DIY, there is a premade product called Pumpkin Fresh.

Keep your jack o' lanterns cool, but don't let them freeze. If you plan to light up your pumpkins before Halloween, use electric lights because they won't heat up and dry out your pumpkin. You can always use electric lights before Halloween and then pop real candles in on Halloween night if you want to capture the fire tradition.

• EXERCISE 3 •
Old-World Turnip Jack-o'-Lanterns

Turnip jack-o'-lanterns are unexpectedly creepy. An older tradition, they're a great way to honor the beloved dead, which is a main theme of the witch's sabbat of Samhain. Before the Irish came to America, they carved turnips into jack-o'-lanterns to welcome the spirits of dead relatives and at the same time ward the household against dark spirits that might be afoot on Halloween night. It didn't take long for the Irish immigrants to realize that pumpkins are larger and much easier to carve. Old-world turnip jack-o'-lanterns might be a bit tougher to carve since you start with a solid vegetable instead of a hollow one, but the results are wicked cool enough to make trying it worth your while.

First, let's discuss the vegetable in question so that you can be sure to find the right thing at the grocery store or produce stand. I went to the store looking for turnips and was disappointed because what I found in the produce section were little white spherical roots, smaller than a baseball, labeled "turnips." I was unsatisfied, to say the least. I had seen photos and old paintings of these turnip jack-o'-lanterns, and these didn't look right at all—plus, how the heck was I going to hollow out and carve this little thing, much less fit a tealight candle inside? Right next to the turnips were some bigger root veggies labeled "rutabagas." I thought, "Well, if I can't find bigger turnips, maybe I can use a rutabaga in a pinch." I bought neither and went home to do more research. Here is what I discovered.

There are several vegetables that they used in Ireland to light up Halloween night: potatoes, a member of the beet family called a mangelwurzel, and turnips, also known as Swedes or, in Scotland, neeps. The Swedish name for that same vegetable that the Irish call a turnip is "rottabaggar," which is the vegetable that in America we call a rutabaga! Were my Irish ancestors pointing out the rutabagas to me in the grocery store? I like to think so. If you're in Europe, you probably already know what vegetable to carve for your turnip jack-o'-lanterns, but if you're in America, drop that sad little turnip and reach for a rutabaga instead.

To make your own terrifying turnip jack-o'-lantern, you'll need the biggest turnip you can find, a sharp chef's knife, and your choice of a chisel, hammer, and spoon combo or a melon baller to hollow it out. You'll also need either a very small sharp knife for carving the face or one of those little saws from a pumpkin-carving kit.

Use the knife to cut a flat area on the bottom so it won't wobble while you work. Next, carefully cut the top off of your turnip (you'll put it back on later). Now, depending on how old-school you want to get, you can either attack it with a chisel and hammer to begin hollowing out the turnip or—if you're not against modern tools—try the melon baller, scooping out little bits at a time. Keep going until you have about a ½-inch-thick wall. Set all those good turnip guts aside; you can freeze them and add to soup, stew, or something else.

Now that it's hollow, carving the face is really similar to carving a pumpkin. Draw on the face, and cut it out using a paring knife, steak knife, or a pumpkin-carving saw. Many people add a chimney to the top by just cutting a big hole in it to let the heat of the candle escape. Some also like to drill a hole in each side about an inch from the edge and run a long piece of twine through to create a handle for carrying or creating a hanging display. You can use real candles if you wish, but battery-operated tealights work perfectly for these little jack-o'-lanterns, and they're safer. A candle will cook that turnip, while a battery-operated light will make it last much longer.

I'll be honest, I had heard that these were really hard to do, but I proceeded undaunted, determined to carve a turnip. I used a melon baller to hollow it out, and I highly recommend this method. I found that it wasn't much harder than a pumpkin; in fact, if I could have purchased enough big turnips in my town, I would have carved a whole family of them. I wrapped my carved turnip in plastic wrap and it lasted for a week in my fridge, then I used an LED tealight on Halloween night. I left it on the porch just to see how long it would last, and it was shriveled a little bit about a week later in cool weather (which just made it look creepier), but it was still in pretty good shape.

• EXERCISE 4 •
Witch's Herb Bottles

If you've been to the Halloween store or browsed your local craft store or big-box store, you've seen those cool-looking bottles that look like spell ingredients: bat wings, eye of newt, classic gross witch stuff, right? Classic, yes; gross, not so much. They might sound like horrible dismembered body parts, but they are actually the names of medicinal and magical plants.

In the old days, village wise women and cunning men, also known as witches, used them in their herbalism practices for healing and magic when they served their communities. Their names for ingredients were descriptive so that when they wrote in their journals and herbal manuals, the names were a secret code that kept their formulas a mystery to the untrained eye. Some of these old handwritten formularies vary a bit, but many of the names are pretty standard. Some of these herbs are in your own kitchen—they're the herbs we use every day. They have magical properties, too, and some have weird and witchy names.

Instead of storebought potion bottles, how cool would it be to have labeled bottles full of magical herbs with their witch names? It's pretty easy to do. With some simple labels and bottles, you can turn any shelf in your home into a witch's apothecary!

Gather together your bottles—you might use herb bottles you already have, find some interesting shaped bottles at your local resale or dollar store, or clean and save small bottles and jars throughout the year. Clean them out and paint the lids with some black paint and you're ready to go. You can make your own labels by doing a quick internet search for "public domain Halloween borders" and add them to a label template for printable labels you've purchased at your local office supply store. Alternately, you can arrange them on a page in a graphics or word processing program, print on plain paper, cut apart by hand, and apply with a glue stick or just tape them on if you're using your actual herb jars and want to remove them after Halloween. You can also find predesigned pages of labels online by searching "free printable blank apothecary labels" or purchase printable or preprinted labels from online craft marketplaces; there are lots of options. You can always hand letter the herb names onto the labels if you like.

Now you might be wondering what to put on the labels; don't worry, I've got you covered. Below is a list of some kitchen herbs that have fabulously witchy names. I'm also including the botanical names of each. I made mine with the witch's name and botanical name only, and it looked very cool and mysterious. My Halloween guests had to look up the botanical names on their phones to see what they were.

These witchy herb jars aren't just pretend magic; they're based on the real deal. Will you display them with the actual herbs in your decorative bottles, like I do? That's completely up to you. Don't worry if the bottles are only partially full; after all, witches use their herbs.

KITCHEN HERBS, THEIR OLDE WITCH NAMES, AND THEIR BOTANICAL NAMES

ROSEMARY	ELF LEAF	ROSMARINUS OFFICINALIS
DILL SEED	HAIRS OF A BABOON	ANETHUM GRAVEOLENS
SAGE	TOAD	SALVIA OFFICINALIS
BASIL	WITCH'S HERB OR DEVIL'S HERB	OCIMUM BASILICUM
MUSTARD SEED	EYE OF NEWT	BRASSICA ALBA
CATNIP	CAT'S WORT	NEPETA CATARIA
TARRAGON	DRAGON'S WORT	ARTEMISIA DRACUNCULUS
PARSLEY	DEVIL'S OATMEAL	PETROSELINUM CRISPUM
CORIANDER	STINKDILLSAMEN	CORIANDRUM SATIVUM
DRIED APPLE	FRUIT OF THE UNDERWORLD	MALUS PUMILA
POPPY SEED	BLIND EYES	PAPAVER SOMNIFERUM
CHAMOMILE	BLOOD OF HESTIA	MATRICARIA CHAMOMILLA
FENUGREEK	BIRD'S FOOT	TRIGONELLA FOENUM-GRAECUM

PLANTS OF THE GARDEN, THEIR OLDE WITCH NAMES, AND THEIR BOTANICAL NAMES

YARROW	BLOODWORT	ACHILLEA MILLEFOLIUM
FOXGLOVE	BLOODY FINGERS (POISONOUS! WEAR GLOVES IF HANDLING)	DIGITALIS PURPUREA
MULLEIN	GRAVEYARD DUST	VERBASCUM THAPSUS
SPANISH MOSS	BAT'S WOOL	TILLANDSIA USNEOIDES
DANDELION	SWINE SNOUT	TARAXACUM OFFICINALE
VALERIAN	BLOODY BUTCHER	VALERIANA OFFICINALIS
MORNING GLORY	BINDWEED	IPOMOEA PURPUREA
HOLLY LEAVES	BAT'S WINGS	ILEX AQUIFOLIUM L.
KNOTWEED GRASS	SPARROW'S TONGUE	POLYGONUM AVICULARE
ACONITE	WOLF'S BANE	ACONITUM NAPELLUS
GROUND IVY	CAT'S FOOT	GLECHOMA HEDERACEA

• • • •

WITCHY TIP: These are not kitchen herbs. Some are poisonous or may have insecticide on them. If you don't know what you're doing, don't ingest herbs not meant for culinary use.

82

two

• EXERCISE 5 •

Mini Pumpkin Tealight Holders

These mini pumpkin candleholders look classy when grouped on a table or scattered throughout the house; you could even place them around your jack-o'-lanterns. Magically, both pumpkins and gourds are great for prosperity, protection, love, and intuition. The year my daughter got married, instead of planting our usual garden of tomatoes and zucchini, we filled our garden beds with white mini Baby Boo pumpkins. Yes, they're technically gourds, but we all call them pumpkins, don't we? My husband, Dan, watered them every day, and our yard started to look like *The Day of the Triffids*, that old horror movie about killer plants!

We ended up making about a hundred of these mini pumpkin candleholders for my daughter's October wedding to enchant the reception hall with the magic of prosperity and love. These are easy to make and look amazing. Her wedding was October 3, and we still had mini pumpkin tealights that looked decent at all our houses that year for Halloween. While I can't guarantee that yours will last as long, depending on climate and temperature, of course, you can do these up to a week in advance and they should last pretty well in a cool, dry location.

This is a two-person project. You'll need some mini pumpkins, a drill, and a 1½-inch saw bit. Grab a pair of heavy leather work gloves—they're inexpensive at the hardware store. You'll also need some tealight candles or battery-operated tealights if you prefer. We found that using real candles didn't really shorten the life of these pumpkins. Since all the heat basically just goes right up, it doesn't affect the pumpkin much.

I suggest doing these outside because it can get messy. Begin by breaking off the stem of the pumpkin so that it won't interfere with the saw blade. You can use a pair of pliers to easily snap off the stem. Set your pumpkin on a level surface; we just did ours on the ground. One person wears the leather gloves and holds the pumpkin steady, and the other person operates the drill on low. Attach the hole cutter to your drill and set it on the lowest speed. Center the cutter over the middle of the pumpkin and press down a bit to push the teeth into the pumpkin *before* you turn on the drill. Pulse the drill a couple of times through the top of the pumpkin—it's just a pumpkin, not a big block of wood, so it doesn't take much. You can also cut the hole by hand; the drill is much faster if you have many to do. Use a spoon and scrape any loose seeds or strings. Now drop in your tealight candle and prepare to light up the night!

Work some Samhain magic into your pumpkin candle-holders by drawing magical symbols on the bottoms of them in permanent marker or carving symbols into your tealight candle before lighting. You can also add a couple drops of oil or a sprinkle of herbs to your tealight. Try cinnamon, patchouli, or pine. For protection and good energy, use rosemary, lavender, or frankincense. Boost intuition with bay or nutmeg.

• EXERCISE 6 •
Doorway-Guarding Wreath

Is it a decorative wreath or a magic talisman for good luck for your doorway or gate on Halloween night? It's both!

Halloween is tied to superstitions about doorways and gateways; after all, it's the time of the year when the door to the otherworld cracks open enough for spirits to venture through. We've talked about the jack-o'-lantern as a protective talisman according to folklore, and we see them usually next to doorways and gates and borders. There are also other folklore traditions to keep dark energies at bay, especially on Halloween night. I love the idea of adding some of these elements to a decorative Halloween wreath to create a beautiful decoration that also functions as magical protection and brings good luck.

If you're not a very crafty person or if you already have a Halloween wreath that you love, you can easily just tuck some of these items for magical protection into any wreath using twist ties, ribbon, or a spot of hot glue. If any of the items looks great with your wreath, feel free to make them a focal point, but if there's a small item in my suggestions for protective folklore talismans that you really want to use but it doesn't go with your wreath, you can tuck it down under something else or in the back of the wreath so it's still there but secret and unseen.

If you're making your wreath from scratch, first you'll need a plain grapevine wreath like the kind you can find at craft stores. Artificial or dried flowers to match your style are a nice touch—you can go with colorful mums, black roses, or anything in between. I suggest finding some Halloween pretties like pumpkin picks or some preserved or artificial autumn leaves. Choose a roll of 2½-inch-wide decorative Halloween ribbon. Loosely arrange the items on the wreath in your shopping cart just to see if you have enough to fill it in, and make sure it all looks good together. As you shop, think about the meanings behind those bats, ravens, and pumpkins that we explored at the beginning of chapter 2. You'll also need a hot glue gun and some hot glue sticks to put it all together.

Now let's talk about magical talismans you can add to your wreath either in an obvious way or covertly, whatever your style. You don't have to add them all or you can load it up. Pick and choose the ones that appeal to you or that you can easily find.

- Rice added to an orange or black organza bag distracts spirits and brings blessings of abundance.
- Salt purifies and is great for doorway protection; it can also be included in a wreath by adding it to a small organza bag.
- A small bell. The ringing of a bell is known to clear away negative energies.

- Mustard seed protects your home from physical and spiritual danger. I think it would be cool in a tiny jar or bottle that could be hot-glued or tied onto your wreath. Decorate it with a label that says "Eye of Newt," its classic witch name.

- A mirror, either an obvious one or a small hidden one, offers great magical protection and deflects bad intentions or negative energy. Make sure you attach it well so it doesn't fall off.

- A safety pin is a classic bit of magical protection folklore that's easily hidden amongst your wreath elements.

- A small bit of real silver, like a silver charm, bead, or even a bit from a broken chain, can also be easily stashed amongst the fall leaves.

- For some magic additions that look like they came right out of *The Blair Witch Project* or an ancient cottage on the moors, tie sticks to form equal-armed crosses together with either natural material like raffia or red string; this is classic folklore protection magic. Rowan wood, ash, or blackthorn are all ideal, but use whatever you have; it's the intention that makes the magic.

- Another classic witch trick is a hag stone, which is a stone with a natural hole in it. It's great for protection magic and also shields against nightmares.

- A sprig of fresh rosemary or a sprig of juniper tied somewhere on your wreath adds extra magical protection for your doorway.

- Last but not least, attach a bit of iron, like an iron nail. Iron is well known to be protective against ghosts, spirits, and the dark fey (whom we also call "the good people" so as not to offend).

• • • •

Once you've decided how to arrange all your decorative and magical pieces on the wreath and you're happy with the look, you can hot-glue them on. When your wreath is finished, display it proudly as it adds ambiance and magic to your Halloween.

three

CELEBRATE WITH
TRICKS AND TREATS

We all think of Halloween as being a scary holiday; after all, it's based on an ancient festival of the dead and otherworldly beings who we needed to hide from behind masks. It also marked the beginning of the hardest season for ancient people, when the future seemed uncertain, so it makes sense that the aspect of fear would still survive today. The truth is, many people enjoy a small scare. Of course, different people have different levels; being a little bit scared can actually be good for us sometimes.

Scary movies make our hearts pound because our minds identify with what the people in the story are going through. Haunted house events have become very popular during the Halloween season and can be much like an amusement park ride, giving us a sense that we're in danger, but in reality we seldom are. We tell scary stories around the campfire, hearkening back to our ancestors, who felt safer around the fire at night but still wanted to talk about their fears. Modern versions of these campfire stories are creepypastas, which are supernatural scary stories copied and pasted on the internet. Scaring the bejeezus out of teens and tweens all over the world, these stories seem more real because they're on a website.

What all of these things have in common is the big scare (which makes you feel unsafe) and then the big relief at the end (which makes you feel as if you have actually survived something scary and lived to tell the tale). It doesn't matter that you were never in any real danger; your brain reacts as if you were, and that feeling of relief and the rush fills us with endorphins and can ultimately boost our confidence and make us emotionally stronger. This is why we often laugh after recovering from a safe scare. Witches know that fully experiencing our emotions can give us power and increase our magic. Experiencing a strong emotion, including fear, is one of the ways that practitioners of chaos magic charge magical sigils to manifest change. In this way, fear can be a positive tool.

This urge to scare and be scared may be what kept pranks going as a part of Halloween for so long. Committing a prank and getting away with it is a form of the same psychological triggers as the safe scare, although with pranking there is a real chance of getting caught, and in more serious pranks getting arrested or even accidentally

Witches know that fully experiencing our emotions can give us power and increase our magic. In this way, fear can be a powerful tool.

hurting someone. We have, of course, traded the tricks for treats when we celebrate modern Halloween, at least for the most part. The promise of a sugar rush is the only thing to stop those pranksters from wreaking havoc like back in the old days.

The term "trick or treat" is now considered the proper greeting when you show up on a doorstep on Halloween. While it may evoke the older meaning of a bit of friendly extortion, it has since transformed into a fun refrain that says, "Here we are in our awesome costumes; may we please have some candy?" Even though I know the roots of the term, it makes me sad when kids show up and just hold out their bags, looking blankly without saying "trick or treat." I'm happy to report that most of the kids who come to my house do sing it out with a big grin and also reply with a happy "thank you" when I drop a handful of candy in their buckets and bags. Occasionally kids will have a joke to share. I wonder if they know that's a tradition that goes back to the sixteenth century? In Scotland the tradition still continues, and the etiquette states that children must earn the treat with a joke or some kind of party trick.

Who Do You Want to Be?

I love seeing the costumed kids coming to my door, and I also just love dressing up myself. Whether it's going to a private party, the local witches' ball, or just answering my door, it's not Halloween for me without a costume. Some years I plan something elaborate; other years I cobble together something creative out of what I already have, depending on time and finances. Costumes were a part of this holiday back when it was Samhain, after all, and people dressed strangely to keep from looking like humans while out on the night of spirits. There's just something about wearing masks, costumes, and makeup. Most of the time it's important to just be yourself...but on Halloween you can be anyone you want!

I recall being in grade school and going to a big after-school Halloween party they had for us little kids in a gym at a local high school. I was dressed as Batgirl. It was one of those old-fashioned vinyl costumes with the plastic mask that covered your whole face and twisted up your hair in the elastic. The costume was a black smock-type thing with the bat logo emblazoned across the chest and a yellow utility belt printed on it. As costumes went, it was okay, but the transformation inside was what counted. They had a little haunted house set up for the kids. Looking back, I'm sure it wasn't that scary—after all, it was for a bunch of kids—but I was a shy, socially awkward little kid full of anxiety. Wearing another persona that day gave me the courage I didn't always have. I mean, Batgirl wouldn't be afraid to go into that haunted house. So I powered through it, brave and strong like a superhero, my breath fogging up the inside of that plastic mask, but I wasn't about to take it off because it gave me power!

That's the benefit of costumes: we get a chance to try out being someone else. What we wear really can transform us, too. When we dress more professionally, we feel more confident; we shift our role without even knowing it sometimes, depending on how we're dressed.

The power of a costume is definitely transformative. Trying on a different persona for even one night can boost us up. If you've been feeling powerless, dressing as a superhero or the scariest thing in the room might be just what you need. If you want to express your sense of humor or creativity, it's the best time of the year to do that. It can also be a great experience to go in costume as

It's important that we are mindful about all of our choices when choosing costumes, which can either serve for fun, fantasy, and elevating our spirits or can ridicule, stereotype, or stomp down the spirits of others, which is, in turn, a reflection of our own spirit and character. Have fun choosing a persona on Halloween, but also do it thoughtfully because we are all part of the generations who have the opportunity to elevate humanity or drag it down.

a figure that you admire. Whether a rock star, character from your favorite show, or an athlete you look up to, emulating someone else with your costume can help you awaken in yourself some aspects of their personality that you like.

More and more we've been seeing very sexualized costumes. Some adults wear these as a license to dress in a much sexier way than they normally would—after all, "it's not me, it's the costume." These costumes have brought much controversy and debate. At the end of the day, pick a costume for you, not anyone else, and choose something that makes you feel empowered or allows you to express yourself.

While we're thinking about expressing ourselves through costume, let's consider that today we've had opportunities to have more open discussions about different cultures, races, sexuality, and religions than ever before. Our society is slowly learning to be more caring about the marginalized people of our world. As this happens, we become more conscious about some costume choices as well because we begin to realize that the things we do can hurt other people. We are witnessing a pivotal time in history as the human race becomes more emotionally and socially evolved, even if a loud minority prefers it didn't. It's important that we are mindful about all of our choices when choosing costumes, which can either serve for fun, fantasy, and elevating our spirits or can ridicule, stereotype, or stomp down the spirits of others, which is, in turn, a reflection of our own spirit and character. Have fun choosing a persona on Halloween, but also do it thoughtfully because we are all part of the generations who have the opportunity to elevate humanity or drag it down.

Time to Trick-or-Treat

When it comes to trick-or-treating, there are many things to consider regarding safety. These might seem like no-brainers, but it's always a good idea to go over a checklist because it's easy to get excited and forget something important. Witches usually use common sense combined with magic to manage life's challenges, and keeping our kids safe is no exception.

- Children out trick-or-treating should be accompanied by an adult.

- Older kids who feel like they don't need adult supervision should always travel in packs—there's safety in numbers. Go over general safety rules with them.
- Bring a fully charged cell phone just in case there's an emergency.
- Many costumes are black and hard to see, so don't take chances: having everyone use a flashlight, glow sticks, or reflective tape can make everyone more visible to cars.
- Double-check costumes and costume elements to make sure the person wearing the costume can easily see and that there are no tripping hazards.
- Add a layer of magical protection to your kid's Halloween attire by including a tiny pinch of sea salt in their shoes (you can toss a small pinch in their treat bag too). You can also include wearing protective stones like black onyx, tourmaline, moonstone, or bloodstone.
- Stay on well-lit streets.

- Never go inside anyone's home.
- Kids should be warned to never get in a car with a stranger during Halloween or any other time.

When we were kids, our parents went through our treats and always tossed out any candy that was unwrapped or partially unwrapped when we got home, and it's not really a bad idea. These measures are a precaution, of course; that whole tainted candy thing is actually an urban legend. There have never been any verified reports of random people putting poison in candy to hand out. The only incident of a poisoning was because a man had put poison in his own child's candy on Halloween and used the holiday to disguise his heinous crime. If people really want extra peace of mind, the local hospitals usually offer free candy X-rays on Halloween night. Almost all reports of sharp items being put into candy end up being hoaxes and were put there by the people themselves. Some people feel that the X-rays give them security; that being said, I've never had a bag of candy X-rayed.

Neighborhood trick-or-treating is my favorite, but in recent years a new addition called trunk-or-treat has been added to the events hosted for children. Hosted by churches or schools, usually before Halloween, participants park their cars in a parking lot, open their trunks, and decorate them for Halloween. Costumed kids walk from trunk to trunk collecting candy. These events often have carnival games and contests too, making it a festive time. Most of the people passing out candy at these events register in advance, which adds an extra perceived level of accountability. Many people attend trunk-or-treat events and then still go out Halloween night around the neighborhood. Neighborhood trick-or-treating is a tradition that I sincerely hope never fades away.

(Haunted) House Rules

If you're staying home to haunt your front yard and pass out candy, there are also some safety concerns to keep in mind. Even if your house looks scary, it shouldn't be dangerous. Any decorations should be placed far enough away from the path so that they can't trip anyone. If you have jack-o'-lanterns near the walkway where costumes will be floating by, consider electric lights because you can't be sure that all costumes are not flammable. If you're using outdoor lights and other things that have power cords, make sure that they are all plugged in correctly and that you're not overloading any extension cords. Ensure that electric cords are arranged in a manner that won't trip anyone by using gaffer tape or duct tape or a small outdoor rug over the top of them. Be sure to sweep the sidewalk that day because if leaves are slightly damp, they can cause people's feet to slip out from under them. I also like to walk the perimeter of my Halloween yard display on Halloween morning with a quartz crystal point and visualize it casting positive energy around the area, with the intention that all guests that evening have fun and are safe.

The well-known but unwritten rule of trick-or-treating is that if your porch lights are on or a pumpkin is lit, you have candy to share. Some people have age limits on which trick-or-treaters they'll give candy to; I personally think that's ageist. If you're young at heart enough to dress up and come to my house saying "trick-or-treat," you're leaving with some candy. I had teens taking selfies at my house last year; they were polite, respectful, and delighted not to be turned away. That being said, older trick-or-treaters should check the laws in their areas...

yes, I'm not even kidding. Some cities have banned older kids from participating in trick-or-treat! A friend of mine recently overheard someone in the Halloween aisle complaining that "adults and older kids have stolen Halloween away from little kids!" To which I laughed and said, "If you look at the history of the holiday, you'll see that's just not true at all." If you have older kids and live in a city that doesn't allow them to trick-or-treat because of their age, encourage them to help work the door and pass out candy. It can be really fun, and they can still dress up and eat candy!

Special Treats

A recent development in Halloween traditions is the Teal Pumpkin Project. Participants place a teal pumpkin (or a sign with a teal pumpkin on it) and a separate container of non-food treats for kids who have special needs like food allergies or childhood diabetes so they can celebrate Halloween too. It's easy to participate if you feel moved to do so.

I did it for the first time this year. Last year we had a little boy with a teal pumpkin bucket trick-or-treating at our house, and that kid was the shining light of our

Halloween—he was having the best time and loved all our decorations. I told his mom all I had was candy since I recognized the teal pumpkin and realized that he might have special dietary restrictions. She explained that he gets to eat a few and they had a bag of toys at home that he can trade in the rest of the candy for. This year when he came to my house, though, that little guy got a special non-candy treat that he got to keep!

Honestly, it's so easy to grab a couple bags of little cheap plastic toys from the dollar store. I had treat bags that included a Halloween button, pencil, glow bracelet, and spider ring. Since most kids want candy anyway, I didn't need many non-candy treats. I'll keep the leftover toys in a bag with my decorations until next year. Teal Pumpkin Project cost for toys: $5.00; happy kids on Halloween: priceless!

Here's a quick kitchen witch's
trick to give your pets a magical
Halloween blessing of protection.
Put three drops of olive oil in the
palm of your hand and rub your
palms together vigorously as you
imagine golden light building up.
Now use your hands to lovingly
pet your dog or cat and tell them,
"You are blessed, protected, and
safe." Now give them a treat.

Pets on Halloween

Many people like to get their pets into the act by dressing them up. I've never had a furry member of my family that was okay with this, so I can't offer much advice in this area. If you and your dog agree that he's Superman, by all means, go there. If you do costume your pet, please consider their feelings and safety, watch them closely, and if they seem uncomfortable or unhappy, take the costume off.

Make sure that you don't leave pets outside, even if they usually stay in the yard. Troubled individuals might bother or even steal or harm them using Halloween as an excuse. Many shelters don't allow black cats to be adopted in October as a precaution, but more often to prevent people from adopting a black cat as a prop for their Halloween costume or party, only to abandon them later. The Pagan/Witch events and groups I've attended actually raise money to support no-kill animal shelters because of course we absolutely do not sacrifice black cats or any other animals; we respect animals. Regardless, keep your pets indoors on Halloween; at the very least, the large number of people out and about can stress out your pet.

While your pets are inside, people ringing the doorbell constantly can also stress them out, and there's also the factor of the door being opened and closed constantly. Some pets don't have a problem with trick-or-treaters, but if your cat likes to bolt out the door or your dog gets agitated easily, it can help to find a quiet room where they can hang out with their food and water. Natural remedies for stress like herbal remedies or pheromones from your vet or pet store can help them relax. Playing soothing music in the room can help too. Our cats ignore the door, but our dog gets very stressed out when the door is swinging constantly. Our solution was to give our dog a safe space inside, and we set up on the porch to pass out candy.

Speaking of treats, watch out for your chocolate, which is toxic to dogs and cats! It's best to keep all the Halloween candy where they can't get it and pick up some appropriate treats for your critters instead. Other things to watch out for are pumpkins and decorative corn, which aren't toxic in moderation but when used for decorations may have small amounts of mold that can make pets very sick if they eat them. Candles should be kept out of reach to prevent burns; if your pet likes to chew on cords, that's another thing to consider when decorating. Also, don't leave glow sticks lying around where the dog can chew them up. The liquid isn't toxic, but it will make your dog very unhappy, and they could swallow big chunks of plastic.

Halloween Movie Night

A popular way to spend Halloween is by having a movie night. Early paranormal and horror films helped to influence how we celebrate Halloween. Universal Pictures and Hammer Studios created some of the classic horror movies that inspired tons of Halloween costumes in the 1950s and '60s. These two studios are to horror films what Marvel and DC are to comic books. Many people prefer one or the other and some appreciate both, but either one would be fun to watch on Halloween movie night.

Universal monsters include Boris Karloff's square-headed Frankenstein's monster and his bride, Bela Lugosi as Dracula, and Lon Chaney Jr. as the Wolf Man; these films were heavy on budget and scares for the time, but they're not gory. Many Halloween costumes and decorations during the time when trick-or-treating entered its heyday were based on these characters, and we still see them today.

Enter Hammer Studios, who came on the scene a bit later and reintroduced these movie monsters in full color, taking full advantage of color film with bright red blood and guts. Hammer horror films were provocative, gory, and often included themes of the supernatural, including dark cults and Satanism.

Over the years we witches have taken some flack due to our portrayal in film. Many movies enforce negative stereotypes that basically paint all witches and magic users as evil cultists, but people should always remember the difference between reality and movies, and these movies are meant to be all in good fun. The Hammer films cast greats like Peter Cushing and Christopher Lee. Hammer forged a new generation of horror movies to emulate in costume, sexier and bloodier than ever before. Whether you prefer Universal's lavish black-and-white classics like *Frankenstein*, *Wolf Man*, and *Dracula* or Hammer's blood-soaked, scantily clad versions of these monster movies, the classics are always fun for Halloween movie night films.

In the late 1950s through early '70s we saw many other studios producing horror. William Castle directed and produced many classic horror films, including the Vincent Price classic *House on Haunted Hill*. Castle was the producer of *Rosemary's Baby*, which was a great example of a successful film in the genre during that time, as was Hitchcock's psychological thriller *Psycho*.

Indie films like George Romero's *Night of the Living Dead* breathed new life—as well as more social commentary—into horror. Romero is the father of modern zombie culture, including film, TV, and comics. A zombie costume is probably one of the easiest go-to last-minute Halloween costumes of all time. These old horror classics usually air on television and are featured on streaming services in the month of October.

Many people also love watching parodies of these classic horror films on Halloween, taking the opportunity to laugh at fear with films such as *Young Frankenstein* or *Dracula: Dead and Loving It* or *Sean of the Dead*. Back in the 1950s through the '80s there were local weekly TV shows presented by comedic gothically styled hosts who introduced these classic films, the most famous being Vampira and later Elvira, Mistress of the Dark, who has become a Halloween icon in her own right. *The Wizard of Oz* is another film I remember watching around Halloween as a kid because it aired in October. I looked forward to that every year! Many Halloween costumes and décor were inspired by this movie since its release in 1939 forged much modern Halloween iconography.

Which came first, Halloween or Halloween movies? Both, actually. While some films influence the celebration of modern Halloween, other movies wouldn't have existed without Halloween. The forerunner of the holiday horror movie genre, *Halloween,* directed by John Carpenter, is a standout example. It nods to Hitchcock by using light and angles to create tension, a modified William Shatner mask, and a simple methodical score by John Carpenter himself. If you watch the sequel, *Halloween II*, please take the bit about Samhain (mispronounced in the film as Sam Hain, like it's a guy named Sam) with a grain of salt. As a witch, it always gives me the entire eyeroll/snicker/cringe combo, but in fairness there was some erroneous information about Celtic history and folklore circulating back then and they had set about to make a horror film, not a scholarly study, so I forgive them.

Other films from modern times that took their inspiration from Halloween (instead of the other way around) include one of my all-time favorites, *The Nightmare Before Christmas*. It's more family friendly than the standard horror fare and can fulfill both Halloween and Christmas/ Winter Solstice entertainment, which is appreciated by those of us who are loathe to surrender Halloween to Thanksgiving and Christmas. This is a movie you can watch all throughout the holidays and get your Halloween fix without anyone giving you a hard time about it.

The Legend of Sleepy Hollow has been associated with Halloween ever since the holiday became widely celebrated in the United States. I just love Tim Burton's version, even though it doesn't accurately depict the original story by Washington Irving. There is also a silent film version, a Disney animated version that always aired near or on Halloween, and now there's a TV series inspired by the characters. I'm going to blow your mind here: although it's often associated with Halloween, in the original short story Halloween has no mention at all, and it's not a jack-o'-lantern that the horseman throws at Ichabod Crane, it's an uncarved pumpkin that Crane believes is the horseman's actual head!

Many artists began to depict it as a jack-o'-lantern once Halloween and pumpkin carving took off in colonial America, but the original illustrations from early publications clearly show an uncarved pumpkin.

If you plan to honor Halloween with a movie night, today there are tons of Halloween movies to choose from. Some people just love any horror movie on Halloween, but there are also many films that specifically reference Halloween such as *The Addams Family* and *Hocus Pocus*; even sci-fi cult film *Donnie Darko* has Halloween themes. Whatever your choice, motion pictures can be a great part of Halloween tradition; they are stories told by technology instead of by the hearth or bonfire. We see the world of film, having first contributed to the celebration, is now taking its inspiration from the celebration, so it has come full circle.

Haunted House Attractions

I've worked as a designer and actor in a couple professional haunted houses over the years, and I've attended them, too; it's good scary fun on both sides of that plastic cleaver! Many people will say that a guy in a scary mask jumping out at you with a chainsaw has nothing to do with the celebration of Samhain, and on many levels that's true. Samhain is a reverent time, so this is one of the places where Samhain and Halloween diverge; being scared for the secular celebration of Halloween has became part of the tradition. That being said, the enjoyable rush of surviving a scary experience can be transformative, and we can learn a lot about our shadow side from trying such an experience.

• • • •

WITCHY TIP: To magically awaken your courage, wear bloodstone or onyx and sprinkle some thyme in your shoes or pockets.

The first thing you need to know about these attractions is that as scary as they are, they're safe. Not all haunted houses are the same. Before choosing one to attend, consider checking their website to see what kinds of scares to expect and recommended ages to attend so you can choose one appropriate for your group. (Yes, do bring a group; it's much more fun that way.)

Some haunted houses are scarier than others. If you're new to these experiences, you might wish to start with one that has less scary and graphic attractions. Keep in mind that fog machines and strobe lights are often used; people with medical conditions affected by these should consider avoiding these attractions. Dress in comfortable, practical clothing and shoes; you'll probably be standing in line outside and stumbling around in the dark. About waiting in that long line—the earlier you go in October,

Haunted houses are a great way to experience an amazing art form up close and personal.

the shorter the lines will be, but many attractions have characters walking around outside so it's still entertaining while you wait.

These events are full of wonderfully dedicated, creative people, including the conceptual designers, costumers, makeup artists, and actors. Professional haunted houses are some of the last bastions of the craft of practical special effects. With the use of so much digital effects in movies now, this is a great way to experience an amazing art form up close and personal. The actors generally will not touch you, so as you're going into it, remember that it's all in good fun, and even though your heart will race, you're safe.

When I worked at haunted houses, I heard many stories of actors getting punched by guests—an action that will likely get a guest kicked out and possibly charged with a crime. If you're a person that usually has a violent reaction to being scared, this kind of event might not be for you. Acting in one of these events can be really physically challenging, so do your best to be respectful to the actors; they're trying to show you a good scary time. If you or a member of your party gets in there and it becomes too much, you can tell one of the actors that someone needs to leave and they will usually break character and help get them out. Most good attractions train their actors to help if someone is overwhelmed.

If you decide to attend a haunted house, do a bit of research on the specific event first, go with an open mind, and have a good time. When you've made it out, celebrate a bit because you faced your shadows bravely and lived to tell the tale!

Paranormal Investigations

There is another kind of haunted house where you won't find even an ounce of fake blood and no killer clowns: real haunted houses. With the popularity of shows like *Ghost Hunters* and *Most Haunted*, paranormal investigative teams have formed all over. Some of these groups set up public events in October when spirit activity can pick up, and it's a great time to allow guests to participate in an actual investigation.

Most of these events provide some training, and some offer access to equipment such as K2 EMF meters, laser grids, and recording devices. Some will allow you to bring your own equipment as well. Usually space for these is limited, so check your area and see if there are any events locally. When attending this kind of event, the planners already have permission to be in the location, which is often a historical hotel, house, or museum where paranormal activity has been widely reported. If you're new to paranormal investigations, this can be a great opportunity to learn from professionals.

If you prefer to attempt your own investigation, you don't have to spend a ton of money on equipment if you're starting out. Basic gear—like voice recorders and a couple cameras, maybe an inexpensive EMF detector—is a good jumping-off place. If you really want to do it on the cheap, there are even apps you can get for your phone.

Make sure that you know some history about the place you're investigating, and most importantly make sure you have permission from the owners to be there. Get something in writing that includes the date just in case, and make sure you have ID on you as well. Never go alone. You should have at least one other person along for practical safety reasons but also so that you can have any experiences corroborated. Have a fully charged phone, back-up chargers, and extra camera batteries. You'll be walking around in the dark, so a little first-aid kit is a good idea too.

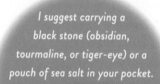

I suggest carrying a
black stone (obsidian,
tourmaline, or tiger-eye) or a
pouch of sea salt in your pocket.

Do some research ahead of time so that you're aware of what kinds of haunting you may find; there are some good beginner's books out there. Always be respectful of any entities present. Keep your head about you and don't panic if things get weird; try to keep an analytical, evidence-based approach. As your witchy friend, I suggest carrying a black stone (obsidian, tourmaline, or tiger-eye) or a pouch of sea salt in your pocket, and wear some frankincense oil to help shield your energy from lower-vibration entities.

Before leaving the site, verbally thank the spirits for their communication and respectfully but firmly tell them the contact has now come to an end. Bring along a bundle of sage and light it, allowing the smoke to waft over everyone who attended the investigation and visualizing any attachments dissolving in the smoke before you head home.

Real versus Fictional Witches

While there are fictional witches, witches themselves are not fictional beings; our spiritual path is just as real as any other faith. We aren't just witches on Halloween or Samhain; our sacred days are part of a wheel that turns with the year as we celebrate the cycles of life and nature.

Because witches are just people, there are often varying opinions on witches and the stereotype of the old woman in a pointed hat on a broom or cackling over a steaming cauldron. Many men and women who are actual witches like to have fun with witch costumes and décor, reveling in the pop culture meta-references. The important thing to remember here is that while the figure of the witch has become a pop culture icon of Halloween, it's also a faith of actual human beings. This should be considered when using this figure to be sure it's done in a kind and respectful way.

Some witches are offended by the green-faced witches used in décor and costumes. The green witch figure came about because of Margaret Hamilton's makeup in *The Wizard of Oz*. Her look was specifically created to take advantage of the brand-new Technicolor it was filmed in. She was such a popular figure when the film came out that soon all Halloween witches shared her emerald tone.

The witches seen on Halloween cards prior to 1939, the year of the film's release, never appear with green skin. Most witches at that time wore many different colored hats and clothing too, but after illustrators got a look at Margaret Hamilton's all-black ensemble in the film, they began to portray all witches wearing fashionable and slimming black.

I myself am not offended by the Wicked Witch; I now think of her as Elphaba from the Gregory Maguire revisionist novel *Wicked* and its sequels. In his books Elphaba is a strong character who, for me at least, reclaims the power of the witch having been labeled as wicked, but is really just human and trying to manage the difficult social and political climate in Oz. Her green skin in his novels is something that sets her apart, challenges her, and eventually empowers her, something that many real witches can understand as a metaphor for not always fitting in.

The figure of an old, ugly witch also offends some modern witches. Unfortunately, our society has come to view age as a bad thing, and we prize beauty above wisdom all too often, which makes the image of the ugly hag witch an insult to real witches. Non-witches should consider this when decorating or costuming. That being said, the figure of the old witch should not be considered evil; in fact, she may be seen as the Crone aspect of the Goddess who is prevalent during the dark part of the year, the season when all things begin to sleep beneath the earth, watched over by the loving embrace of the grandmother of nature. Witches and non-witches can consider embracing the idea of older women as teachers with power and kindness instead of the old lady out to get you.

If anyone wonders why witches can be sensitive this time of the year, people need only consider that historically people have died after being accused of witchcraft. I personally did a lot of research into this for my role in a college production of *The Crucible*. In more recent times witches have lost their jobs, lost custody of their

TIP 6
Harvest of Apples

Apples have been associated with Halloween traditions since the earliest times. Games like bobbing for apples and "snap apple"—catching an apple on a string with your teeth—were usually played at Halloween celebrations. Sometimes the game was made even more challenging (and dangerous) by tying apples onto pieces of wood with burning candles on them! The Cornish feast of Allantide on October 31 is well known as an apple festival featuring such a game.

Including apples in your Halloween celebration carries energy from the past as well as magical symbolism of immortality, love, and healing. Some options can include apple beverages, baked apples, or caramel/candy apples with natural sticks in them to add extra witchy appeal.

children, and been victims of vandalism, all because of the negative stereotypes of their misunderstood nature-based faith. If anyone is in doubt about how to treat a witch with courtesy on Halloween (or any other time of the year), please consider that it's all about context. One need simply insert the name or figure of the member of any other faith; if that seems unkind to another faith, then it likely would also be unkind to a witch.

Oh—also, please don't use the word "witch" as a substitute for a rhyming word that you might use to insult a woman. Really, please don't.

Community Celebrations

If you're looking for a Halloween celebration during the month of October, you can usually find something fun to do no matter what your taste is. In addition to trick-or-treating and haunted houses, many communities have fall and harvest festivals and Halloween-themed parades, shopping events, dances, pumpkin-carving contests, wine tastings—there are lots of fun things to do during the month of October.

Fall festivals can be a great place to pick up produce, jams, local honey, and even baked goods from local farmers and gardeners. For people who don't garden themselves, this can be a great way to connect with the spirit of the land and the harvest. Eating locally grown food is better for the environment because it hasn't been shipped across the country, and often you're buying it right from the person that grew it with their own hands; there's a connection to the basics of life that nourishes the soul.

These festivals are also an opportunity to connect with the local community, listen to live music, and take a break from the daily grind. Some communities do huge Halloween parades with costumed people, music, and floats. There are also some towns that do big Día de los Muertos parades and street parties with gigantic skeletons, street food, music, and dancing.

Another suggestion that people might not think of is to check in with your local high schools and colleges to see what's coming up in their theater. Many local theaters schedule plays for Halloween such as *Sweeny Todd*, *Little Shop of Horrors*, or *Dracula*. My son was in an October production of *The Legend of Sleepy Hollow* in high school, and those kids did an amazing job. Several parents and

Fall festivals are a great way to connect with the spirit of the land and the harvest.

I helped with costumes and set design, and the drama teacher even called in a friend who's a professional makeup artist. These productions are usually an inexpensive evening and are often pretty good. You can also feel like it's money well spent since you're supporting education and the arts on a local level.

Some towns offer Witches' Night Out events, which can be a lot of fun. Usually they are for the general public and have a street fair vibe. Vendors include local crafters, businesses, food, and (if you're lucky) wine or beer tasting. Everyone dresses up in their finest witch costumes and visits booths and local businesses that often have candy or other freebies to hand out. There's often a band or DJ as well, and some do a costume contest. I attended one with some local witches and we had a blast wearing our pointed hats amongst the partying muggles.

Another option would be Witches' Ball events. Many of these are actually hosted by local Pagan communities and are dinner/dances that are mostly real witches, Wiccans, and Pagans; they're a great way for the magical community to network and enjoy fellowship. Attendants dress in elegant costumes, eat, dance, and there's often auctions or raffles as well to raise money for the local communities. They often donate to local food pantries and animal shelters. My husband and I have brought along non-witches to these events a couple times, and they had a blast.

If you're looking for some fun festivities for Halloween, just do an internet search with your local chamber of commerce or nearby cities. You're bound to find something fun to do that will get you in that Halloween spirit without having to travel too far from home.

• EXERCISE 7 •

Soul Cakes

One of the forerunners of trick-or-treat handouts, these sweet medieval cakes flavored with spices and currants can be decorated with an equal-armed cross or a pentagram. Adding saffron makes you the medieval equivalent of the house that hands out full-sized candy bars, just in case you want to take it to the next level!

There are many versions of soul cakes. I'm sure different households had different versions of these treats to hand out to soulers in exchange for prayers on behalf of their beloved dead. Fairly easy to make, these carry the classic flavors from the old recipes but have been adjusted to appeal to a modern palate and baking techniques.

> 2¾ CUPS FLOUR
> ⅔ CUP GRANULATED SUGAR
> 1 TEASPOON NUTMEG
> 1 TEASPOON GROUND ALLSPICE
> 1 TEASPOON CINNAMON
> ½ TEASPOON GROUND CLOVES
> 1 TABLESPOON BAKING POWDER
> ¾ TEASPOON SALT
> ½ CUP BUTTER (1 STICK) LEFT AT ROOM
> TEMPERATURE 10–15 MINUTES

- 1 CUP CURRANTS OR DRIED POMEGRANATES OR CRANBERRIES (NOT TRADITIONAL BUT YUMMY)
- 2 EGGS
- ½ CUP MILK PLUS SEVERAL TABLESPOONS IF NEEDED
- PINCH OF CRUMBLED SAFFRON OR ¼ TEASPOON OR SO LOOSE, OPTIONAL
- 1 ADDITIONAL EGG YOLK AND ¼ CUP SUGAR FOR TOPS

• • • •

If you're not using saffron, skip the following step. Put a generous pinch of crumbled saffron threads into a small saucepan on low and heat until the scent is released, then pour in the milk and warm it in the pan with the saffron, stirring so it doesn't scald. When the milk becomes yellow and is warm, remove it from the heat and set it aside to cool.

In a large bowl, mix the flour, sugar, spices, baking powder, and salt together using a whisk or a fork. Cut the butter into ½ inch or so slices and add them to the dry ingredients, breaking up the butter in the flour mixture with your fingers or a pastry blender until they are about the size of peas or a bit larger.

Mix in the currants. Next, add the milk (or cooled saffron milk) and mix in to make a soft dough. Add more milk a teaspoon at a time if needed to moisten all the flour mixture.

Roll the dough out on a floured board to about ½-inch thick, and cut out the cakes with a floured biscuit cutter. Cut them as close together as you can and then work the remaining dough together to cut the rest.

The last one can be shaped by hand out of the last of the scraps (this is the one I like to taste when they come out of the oven). Place each cake about 1 inch apart on a greased cookie sheet or one lined with baking parchment. Brush the tops with a beaten egg yolk and sprinkle with a bit of sugar.

Put the trays of cakes into the refrigerator while you preheat the oven to 400 degrees Fahrenheit. Once the oven is hot, use a butter knife to press either an equal-armed cross or a pentagram (five-pointed star) on top of each cake.

Bake for 20 minutes until golden brown. Cool on a wire rack.

Yields about 20 2½-inch cakes.

• EXERCISE 8 •

Caramel Apple Dipping Bar

Apples are a tradition that has been carried through from the Samhain celebrations. Caramel apples were invented in the 1950s as a way to use leftover Halloween caramel candy and have been a fall mainstay ever since. I love caramel apples, but no one at my house wants to eat a whole one, so when I buy them I end up cutting them into slices to share.

Now we like enjoying caramel apples by dipping slices into warm caramel and then rolling or sprinkling them with fun toppings. It's a festive bit of fun deliciousness with a high participation factor.

> 4-5 APPLES WASHED AND DRIED (I LIKE GALA, FUJI, OR HONEYCRISP)
>
> TOPPINGS CAN INCLUDE CHOPPED NUTS, HALLOWEEN CANDY SPRINKLES, SEA SALT, MINI CHOCOLATE CHIPS, COCONUT, MINI MARSHMALLOWS, CRUMBLED GINGER SNAPS, CRUMBLED PRETZELS—LET YOUR IMAGINATION RUN WILD!
>
> SKEWERS FOR EACH APPLE SLICE
>
> PREMADE CARAMEL DIP OR MAKE YOUR OWN WITH 11 OUNCES OF CARAMELS, $1/4$ CUP HALF AND HALF, AND 3 TABLESPOONS MAPLE SYRUP OR PANCAKE SYRUP

Heat caramels, half and half, and syrup on low in a small saucepan, stirring often until melted and blended well. You could also microwave on high in a microwave-safe bowl, stopping it to stir every minute. It takes about 3 to 3½ minutes. Keep going until caramels are melted and everything is mixed in.

To Serve

Slice and core your apples. You can do this using a paring knife or you can use one of those push-down apple slicer/corers. To slow down the browning of the sliced apples, add a half teaspoon of salt per cup of water and soak your apple slices for ten minutes. Drain and rinse, then store in the refrigerator until ready to use. Dry them well before serving.

Skewer each apple slice at one end deep enough so that it's secure. You can either lay them on a tray or place them apple-end up in a tall festive vase or a plastic jack-o'-lantern full of glass gems or marbles to weigh it down. Place toppings in small bowls; the small three-legged cauldron–type dishes used for salsa are great, or you can use a muffin tin with liners to display and serve your toppings. Be sure to provide napkins and little dessert plates for your guests, and enjoy!

TIP 7
The Electric Cauldron

Halloween conjures up images of a witch working up some magic over a bubbling cauldron, a tradition that has been going on at my house since my kids were little. Yes, I'm talking about good old-fashioned kitchen witchery. When you have little kids (or big kids) in the house, the best way to get them to eat something other than candy on Halloween is to keep it simple. I usually break out my slow cooker and fill it with some delicious chili; beans were a big part of Lemuria, the Roman festival of the dead, so chili on Halloween works with tradition. Mostaccioli or soups with Halloween pasta in it are other good options. Slow cooker or modern pressure cooker dishes are hot and ready whenever someone wants it, so it can take stress out of a hectic day. Another great use for your slow cooker would be to serve up some hot mulled wine or apple cider.

• EXERCISE 9 •
Barmbrack:
Irish Fortunetelling Sweet Bread

In Irish *barm* means "bread" and *brack* means "speckled," so barmbrack is speckled bread. It's not just a sweet bread; it's also an old Irish form of divination. Charms are hidden in the bread. Each charm foretells what the future holds for whoever finds it in their slice. In Ireland this delicious tea loaf is served in many households all year without the addition of the charms, but it is especially savored as a treat for Halloween. Some versions use yeast, but this one uses baking soda.

In the old tradition there were many charms baked into this bread to determine fortunes for the upcoming year: a coin for money; a ring for love/engagement; a thimble, button, or a dried pea meant you would remain unmarried; a bit of rag meant poverty; a stick meant unhappy marriage and strife. Many people carry on this tradition today using only a ring and a coin. I love the idea of adding new charms to this tradition: what about a metal bee charm for employment or a raise, a key to predict overcoming obstacles, or a metal sun charm for success?

Of course the charms are wrapped in parchment paper before adding them so that they stand out from the barm and no one breaks a tooth in this tasty fortunetelling game.

3 CUPS MIXED DRIED FRUIT, RAISINS,
   CURRANTS, OR SULTANAS (AKA GOLDEN
   RAISINS)
1¼ CUPS STRONG BLACK TEA MADE WITH
   2 TEA BAGS
1–2 TABLESPOONS WHISKY (OPTIONAL)
1 EGG
2 CUPS FLOUR
1 CUP LIGHT BROWN SUGAR
2½ TEASPOONS BAKING SODA
½ TEASPOON SALT
½ TEASPOON CINNAMON
½ TEASPOON NUTMEG
½ TEASPOON GROUND ALLSPICE
1 TEASPOON CINNAMON
¼ TEASPOON GROUND CLOVES
RING, COIN, AND OTHER CHARMS WRAPPED
   IN BAKING PARCHMENT

• • • •

Soak dried fruit overnight (at least six hours or so) in strong tea; add whisky if you want. Preheat oven to 350 degrees.

Beat the egg and combine it with the fruit and tea mixture. In a separate bowl whisk together flour, brown sugar, baking soda, and spices. Combine the dry and wet ingredients and mix well with a wooden spoon. Pour the mixture into a loaf pan lined with parchment paper. Push the parchment-wrapped charms into the batter at different intervals.

Bake for 1½ hours or until it feels firm to the touch and a toothpick inserted comes out clean. Cool ten minutes, then turn it out onto a wire rack and allow it to cool completely.

Many people say this gets even better after a day, so feel free to make it ahead of time. I make two loaves: one to devour with butter while it's still warm and one to save for company!

• EXERCISE 10 •

Creepypasta Soup

This rich, hearty soup gets its name from the scary online stories of the internet age known as "creepypastas" (derived from "cut and paste"). It's a rich soup with vegetables, sun-dried tomatoes, meatballs, and pasta that rivals chili in popularity at my family Halloween celebrations. I've included vegetarian options for the ingredients as well.

- 2 CANS TOMATO SOUP
- 2 CANS BEEF BROTH (OR SUB VEGGIE OR MUSHROOM BROTH)
- 2 CANS WATER
- ¼ CUP RED WINE (OR TO TASTE)
- 3 GARLIC CLOVES
- 5 SUN-DRIED TOMATOES, DICED
- ½ ONION, DICED
- 1 BAG FROZEN MEATBALLS, BROWNED (OR SUB 1 CAN CHICKPEAS OR KIDNEY BEANS)
- 1 BAG FROZEN MIXED VEGETABLES (I LIKE THE CORN, PEAS, CARROTS, AND BEANS MIX)
- SALT, PEPPER, CRACKED RED PEPPER, AND ITALIAN HERBS TO TASTE
- HALLOWEEN-SHAPED PASTA (OR PASTA OF YOUR CHOICE), COOKED ACCORDING TO DIRECTIONS; ADD RIGHT BEFORE SERVING TO KEEP THE PASTA FROM GETTING MUSHY

Put all ingredients in your slow cooker (except the pasta) and cook for 3–4 hours (20 minutes in a pressure cooker).

• EXERCISE 11 •

Sparking Witch's Brew Punch

This is a nonalcoholic and very simple punch, but it's full of the magic and symbolism of the season. I included pomegranate juice to represent Persephone's journey to the underworld and apple cider as a nod to Halloween apple divination. If you prefer an alcoholic version, there's no reason you can't use hard apple cider instead.

POMEGRANATE JUICE: MAGICAL PROTECTION, PROSPERITY, AND WISDOM

APPLE CIDER: APPLES REPRESENT THE UNDERWORLD, MAGIC, AND DIVINATION

GINGER ALE: LUCK IN LOVE, MONEY, AND SUCCESS—PERFECT FOR THE CELTIC NEW YEAR

• • • •

Blend in equal parts. I like to serve it in a big plastic cauldron with a ladle.

• EXERCISE 12 •

Opal Hush Cocktails

It wouldn't be Halloween at my house without opal hush. This is an old-time cocktail that I'm bringing back! It was described as being served by turn-of-the-century tarot artist Pamela Colman Smith (known to her friends as Pixie) at her fabulous Bohemian parties full of famous artists, theater people, and poets.

The original was made from red claret wine and lemonade from a siphon. Claret is just the old British name for wines from Bordeaux, so if you can't find a bottle that says claret on it, don't worry; I've been known to use a red Bordeaux, Merlot, or Cabernet Sauvignon. You don't have to spend a lot on the wine either; after all, cocktails were invented to mask the flavor of inexpensive spirits.

Like most modern people, I don't own a siphon, so I came up with a recipe using modern methods to include sparkling lemonade for ours. One of these days I'm going to get a proper siphon, but until then this recipe is pretty darned good. I make it in an air-tight plastic pitcher. I suggest making sure you label it or you might upset any straight edges just looking for some nice juice. True story.

1 CAN FROZEN LEMONADE (PLEASE,
   NO POWDERED MIX)
48 OUNCES COLD CLUB SODA
RED WINE: CLARET, BORDEAUX, MERLOT, OR
   CABERNET SAUVIGNON

In a 2-quart pitcher (one that seals will keep it carbonated), add frozen lemonade and fill three-fourths of the way with cold club soda. Be sure it's cold because that helps it keep its fizz. Pour it down the side of the pitcher to release the least amount of bubbles possible. Fill the rest of the way with red wine, and stir very gently. Serve neat (with no ice) in a wine glass.

If you pour it right into the center of your glass, it will create a bit of foam, reminiscent of the "amethystine foam" described as gracing the glasses of Pixie's opal hush.

four

FOLKLORE TRADITIONS, CUSTOMS, AND SPELLS

Halloween has always been a celebration of the realm of spirit—from its mystical beginnings as the Pagan celebration of Samhain to the Middle Ages, when prayers were sent out to help spirits move on, and even into Victorian and Colonial times, when magic and divination were practiced by partygoers for fun. One of the first written references on the topic of these folklore spells and divination techniques is found in the Scottish poet Robert Burns's 1785 poem *Halloween*. Since he was

143

clearly writing about practices that had been a long-standing tradition at that time, we really don't know how far back many of these folk customs go.

Most of the folklore traditions were for the purposes of divination, especially to discover the name of a future spouse or to protect a person or home against malevolent energies, i.e., witchcraft. This always makes me laugh because all those folklore methods to guard against witches are also technically witchcraft! They were doing magic to keep baneful energies away, which most modern witches do all the time, and we even use some of those same techniques.

But in the earlier times many people thought that witches did only harmful magic and that witches got their powers from making a pact with the devil—neither of which is true, of course. They also believed that their own magical precautions to keep harmful magic away were sanctified since they knew they weren't witches themselves. In fact, many people in the old days used charms, chants, and incantations they repeated while performing everyday tasks or for solving specific problems. Many of them were Christianized versions of old Pagan charms

144

and rites. Apparently, in the old days, witchcraft was magic done by someone else but not yourself.

Defining Magic

Every magic user I know has a slightly different definition of what magic is. To me, magic is the art of programming the energy that runs through everything to help us achieve what we want. Some people say it's similar to prayer, and to a certain point I would agree with that. Magic is energy, and it can be used for either positive or negative purposes. Much like fire, which we use to cook our food and keep us warm but can also burn a house down, how you use it is key.

Magic is the power that flows through all living beings, like plants, animals, and you and I, but also non-living matter, like the book you're holding in your hand. A spell is the art of making that energy work for you. To me, the most important thing is that when I work with magic, I don't simply ask the universe for a change and expect it to happen. I see it in my mind, I believe that it can happen, I apply my will and emotions, I raise energy and direct it toward my goals. I don't ask the spiritual

Magic is the art of
programming the energy that
runs through everything to
help us achieve what we want.
Magic is energy...it is the power
that flows through all living
beings, like plants, animals,
and you and I, but also non-
living matter, like the book
you're holding in your hand.
A spell is the art of making
that energy work for you.

energies to make a change *for* me but to help me see the power within myself to make that change.

The Importance of Timing

There are many tricks to working successful magic, and one of them is timing. This would be the reason why, throughout history, so many people have worked magic during Halloween whether they call themselves witches or not. During these power times, people have noticed that the energy is different, and if you can focus your will during these times, things can happen.

There are definitely times of the year when magic can get a boost: during full moons and on the quarters of the year (solstices and equinoxes) and the cross-quarters of the year (the dates that fall directly between the solstices and equinoxes). Samhain/Halloween is, of course, a cross-quarter holiday, falling between the autumn equinox and the winter solstice. Many witches I know celebrate Samhain on Halloween, October 31, but because the solstices and equinox dates vary slightly every year, so does the date between them. Because of this, Samhain is sometimes celebrated on dates near Halloween but maybe not actually on Halloween. This can be helpful for those of us who want to separate these spiritual and secular holidays. Neither is right or wrong, just different depending on the individual's tradition or personal preference.

Halloween is celebrated on October 31 as a set calendar date, no matter which side of the equator you live on, but because Samhain was born as an agricultural harvest celebration, many witches and Pagans who live in the Southern Hemisphere celebrate Samhain on or near May 1. May is autumn in the Southern Hemisphere, and the calendar date of Halloween, October 31, falls in the spring, lining up with the Pagan festival of Beltane, the other sabbat when the veil between the worlds is thin.

Magical Necessities

One might ask what is needed in order to work magic. Again, if you ask a roomful of magic users, you'll get many different answers. I will tell you that although we witches love our magnificent altars full of all the lovely accoutrements, at the end of the day, the most powerful tool that anyone has to make change in our lives is our own mind, spirit, and will.

This is the basis of most folk magic. People weren't casting elaborate circles in magnificent robes, reciting two-page-long incantations, or mixing up the most arcane ingredients known to humankind—not that there's anything wrong with all that. The pomp and circumstance can create a very magical state of mind indeed. But in folk magic traditions people were wearing their everyday clothing, working with simple items from around the house or garden, and applying the concepts of sympathetic magic to make their lives a bit better, and oftentimes it worked.

Many of us who work with magic can apply the folk magic concept that sometimes less is more into our rich and varied magical practices. Many people who didn't even consider themselves witches would perform some of these bits of magic, especially during Halloween, in order to dip a toe into the world of mysteries in hopes of effecting change or gaining insight in a sometimes difficult world. After all, there are times when anyone can sure use a bit of quick magic!

Sympathetic Magic

Sympathetic magic is the basis of much of the folk magic that we see in traditional Halloween spells. It is also called imitative magic and works under the principle that, through magic, a similar thing not only can be connected to another similar thing, it can affect that thing. For example, in primitive times a shaman would paint images of the tribe having a successful hunt to ensure that it would happen.

If the idea of connecting one thing to another seems silly, consider your own talismans that are connected to something: treasured photographs, heirlooms, keepsakes, or even the business card of someone you hold in esteem. Do these things hold importance to you because of the

There are times when anyone can sure use a bit of quick magic!

connection that they have to a person or event? Now think of how you would feel if those things were damaged. Would you feel upset if you saw a symbol of something or someone that you admired burned in effigy? When your grandmother is sick, do you hold her photograph gently and make a wish for her healing? That's because on some deep mystical level you also feel the ancient concept of sympathetic magic. This tradition of "like producing like" has been documented as being a part of magical traditions and practices used by the Egyptians, Romans, and many ancient cultures.

Practical Magic

I love doing research and discovering more about the world, history, and magic, and I have found a plethora of magic that was used back in the day on Halloween by all kinds of people with different belief systems. I feel like each one is a little treasure—a bit of folklore that connects us all to the mysteries that surround Halloween and Samhain and, in fact, to the entire magical year. The exercises in this section reflect that research paired with my practical experiences as a modern witch.

You don't have to be a witch to use these techniques—anyone can use them.

Grounding, Centering, and Shielding

Before we go on this journey to explore the magic of Halloween, I'll share with you my quick methods for grounding and centering, as well as a simple magic shield you can cast around yourself anytime you want, and it travels with you.

All magic users have methods for grounding, centering, and shielding, so if you have something you prefer to use that differs from mine, by all means feel free to use what you're used to. For people who use more extensive grounding and centering techniques or are used to working in a ritually cast circle, you might find these bare-bones methods more practical to use with the simple folklore magic in this section.

Keep in mind that most of these little folklore spells can also be easily worked into a big Samhain ritual for either a solitary witch or coven or be performed on their own in the tradition of old folk magic practitioners and kitchen witches.

Anyone who is new to the idea of working with magic should know that using grounding and centering techniques is always a good idea before attempting any kind of magic because it helps you approach the work from a place of power and calm. The magic shield is recommended, as it maintains your personal energy and protects it from outside influences. These techniques aren't just for working Halloween magic; they can also come in handy anytime you need to have a stable approach to a situation, balance your energy, or if you ever feel inundated by toxic people or energies. You don't have to be a witch to use these techniques—anyone can use them.

153

four

Basics of Magic:
Grounding and Centering

This is a great two-part exercise to connect your spirit with the earth while finding balance and to align your personal power, which is smart to use before doing Halloween magic or divination (or any kind of energy work). This exercise is done with visualization, which is basically imagining with intention. See it happening in your mind, and your energy will follow.

Grounding

To ground and connect with the energy of the earth, while sitting or standing, breathe deeply in through your nose and out through your mouth. Now imagine roots growing down from the place where your body meets the floor. These roots go down, deeper and deeper, and begin to form a deep connection with the earth itself.

Once your roots are established, an exchange between you and the earth can take place. Any negative or unhealthy energy that you've been carrying around flows down through the roots, where the earth can absorb it and neutralize it, releasing the emotional attachments to the energy and making it into a fresh source of power. The earth is grand and powerful, and this process can take place very quickly.

Now you may draw fresh energy up through your roots and fill your body with it. Feel it filling you with calm, stable power; imagine it filling you to the crown of your head and flowing up to the sky. Now you are grounded and ready to face anything, magic or mundane.

Centering

Now to center your energy and align it properly; this is a really simple and powerful technique. Imagine your personal energy as a radiating light that comes from inside of you and fills the air around you about a foot or so outside of your body. You know how you can feel uncomfortable when someone you don't know or trust stands too close inside your "personal bubble"? Well, it's real, and because that space is actually part of you, we call it your personal energy or aura.

Now put your hand on your belly button. About two inches above it is a part of your energy called your solar plexus chakra; it's the center point of your personal power, your anchor. Simply imagine that personal bubble being pulled in closer to your body and in the direction of your solar plexus chakra, allowing your own center to guide the energy gently inward. Take a deep breath. When you breathe out, visualize your energy expanding outward and naturally aligning back up in perfect harmony between your physical body and your energy system. You are now centered.

. . . .

If you liked this exercise and would like to learn more about your personal energy, I recommend picking up a book with more information about chakras such as *Llewellyn's Little Book of Chakras* by Cyndi Dale, which is an excellent source for more information.

• EXERCISE 14 •

Basics of Magic: Shield of Light

This is a great magical shield that you can use anywhere and anytime. It's a magical way to protect your energy from outside influences or from being drained by outside forces. Use this anytime you feel vulnerable and definitely before undertaking Halloween magic or divination.

A psychic shield is a great tool when the veil between the worlds is thin. I've even used this one while standing in line at the supermarket if someone with uncomfortable vibes gets in line behind me. It's quick, easy, and no-nonsense.

Visualize liquid light flowing down like a fountain over your head, pouring down from the source of the energy of the universe; it is pure power. The light spreads all over you, gleaming as it pours down, pushing any bits of negativity that have been caught in your aura downward. The little specks of darkness are no match for the liquid light. The light pushes all negativity downward until it pours down over your feet and is absorbed in the earth.

TIP 8
Halloween Kale Matchmaking

On Halloween night young men and women performed a ritual to learn who their spouse would be. They went blindfolded into a garden and felt around for a stalk of kale. They would pull the stalks, and it was said that the kale they picked would foretell the attributes of the one they would marry. Was it bitter or sweet? Was it lanky or full and round? If it had a lot of earth clinging to the roots, you would marry someone wealthy; roots clean of dirt meant you would fall for someone with less financial resources.

Feel the light envelop you; as it does, it begins to become a crystalline shield that covers you with its light. It's a suit of armor that moves with you, protecting you from any negative outside forces.

Nutcrack Night Love Customs

Roasting hazelnuts on the fire and divining the future from the results became such a popular activity on Halloween night that it was sometimes called Nutcrack Night. The hazel is one of the sacred Celtic trees and is a symbol of wisdom, knowledge, and inspiration, so it's no surprise that the hazelnut was used in an old Halloween spell to gain otherworldly knowledge.

As was often the case, young adults celebrating Halloween in the old days were most interested in matters of the heart, so the hazelnut spell is yet another of many divination practices to discover one's true love.

To learn which one of the people who have caught your eye is the best match for you, gather together several hazelnuts and light a fire in your fireplace, outdoor fire pit, or grill.

Name one nut for yourself and the other nuts for the love interests in your life, and place them in the fire together. The ones that pop and hop away are not the ones for you; whichever nut ends up closest to yours after they crack from the heat is your best match. You'll be able to go through tough times and remain by each other's side!

A second method would be to test the longevity of your current relationship. This one uses only two nuts, one for each of you. Set them side by side in the embers; if they stay together when they crack and burn up, then you'll be together through thick and thin. Should one or both of them crack and jump away from the other, then it may be a sign of future relationship challenges ahead.

• EXERCISE 16 •

Two Dream Lovers Spells

There are several spells to dream of your true love on Halloween night. When doing dream magic, place a pencil and a piece of paper next to your bed so that, upon waking, you can write down any thoughts, symbols, or feelings you might remember. Getting up to look for something to write on can allow dreams to slip quickly back into the subconscious, where they become hard to retrieve, so being prepared is key. Remember that sometimes symbols in dreams are not obvious, so it's a good idea to consult a dream dictionary for clarity.

Rosemary and Sixpence Spell

A simple spell is to put a sprig of rosemary and a silver sixpence (or any silver coin) under your pillow. According to tradition, your true love will be starring in your dreams that night—or at the very least you will dream of clues to lead you toward meeting them.

The Sleeve-Dipping Ritual

Another classic Halloween spell to dream of your true love is the sleeve-dipping ritual. Dip your sleeve into a pond, well, or other natural source of water. I suggest that if you don't live near natural water and want to try it, some bottled spring water poured on the sleeve somewhere in nature should suffice as long as your intentions are strong.

The shirt should be hung to dry by the fire (or heating vent, for modern people). Then, when you go to sleep, the spirit or "fetch" of your true love is said to appear to turn the shirt so that the other side will dry as well.

I imagine it's most likely that this relatively popular spell from the old days is a dream spell and that the suggestion of expecting help from your future love would cause your subconscious mind to summon up the image in a dream of them turning the shirt. Anyone caught dipping a sleeve into the water on Halloween was found out for working a bit of love magic on this magical night.

• EXERCISE 17 •

Apple Eating Spells

Apples have many magical associations and were considered the fruit of life, which grew in the Celtic faery land of Avalon. Apples are associated with both love and the celebration of Halloween; it stands to reason that there would be many Halloween apple love spells to divine one's romantic prospects. Eating an apple in several very specific ways on Halloween can help you get a glimpse of your future spouse.

Here are some of the magical methods described in classic folk traditions:

- Eating an apple at midnight while brushing your hair will allow you to see your future spouse in the mirror over your shoulder.

- Peel an apple in as long a strip as you can—try to peel the entire apple. Focus on a future full of love as you toss the peel over your shoulder. When you look at the peel on the ground, take note of its shape: it should resemble the initial of either the first or last name of your future spouse.

- We've all heard of the game bobbing for apples; it actually evolved from an older game called snap apple. An apple was suspended from a string, and the players attempted to eat the dangling apple. The first to get a bite would be the first to marry. Here's where the spell comes in: girls would put their apple under their pillow on Halloween night to dream of their future husband.

- A less common apple love spell was to attempt eating an apple while looking in a mirror and walking down the stairs backwards. Not only would this be a great way to sustain a serious injury, but, according to folklore, you would also see your future spouse in the mirror if you did it on Halloween night.

Luggie Bowls Fortunetelling

A Scottish tradition, luggie bowls are a Halloween divination game that uses various bowls. Luggie bowls had a handle on either side like ears, which were known as lugs. Any kind of bowl can be used to reproduce this old tradition.

A person is blindfolded and several—usually three—bowls are placed before them. The contents of the bowls vary, but each contains something that is meant to be symbolic of their possible romantic future. The blindfolded player would then reach out to touch or put a hand inside a bowl. The contents of the bowl they touched would foretell their marital status.

Among the possibilities:

- Clean water meant they would marry in the coming year and could also mean that they would marry a virgin.

- Water with soap in it meant they would marry someone wealthy.

- Dirty water or soil meant they would marry a widow or widower.

- An empty bowl meant there would be no marriage that year or possibly that they would remain a bachelor or old maid.

• EXERCISE 19 •

The Bells Toll House-Clearing Spell

Among many cultures, chiming bells are reputed to ward away baneful spirits and negative energy. The ringing of bells on Halloween is an ancient tradition that may even be related to the legend that the fae folk have an aversion to iron and bells; Celts of old were especially wary of the fey on Samhain. The Romans banged bronze pots together to drive out dark spirits on Lemuria. Later, the traditions carried over to honor the dead saints and comfort the souls in purgatory on All Saints' Day and All Souls' Day.

For this simple house-clearing spell, acquire at least one bell, although you may use several if you wish; any kind of bell will do. Walk through your house on Halloween, starting at the front door and moving counterclockwise throughout each room in the house, ringing bells in each room. In your mind envision the soundwaves as the bells' clearing sounds penetrate every space where it can be heard, breaking up negative energy and repelling astral nasties that may be lurking. When you have completed going into each room and ringing the bells, you may wish to hang at least one bell on your front door to keep out any energies that you don't want.

TIP 9
Voices at the Crossroads

Venture to a quiet crossroads (where two roads meet, making an X) on one of three magical nights: May Eve (Beltane), St. John's Eve (Midsummer), or All Hallows' Eve. You might want to bring a friend along for safety—not from spirits, but it's never safe to travel alone at night.

Put your phones on silent. Make your way there at night after the sun has passed well below the horizon and the sky is as black as pitch, although you may have to wait until the trick-or-treaters are done for the night.

When you arrive at the crossroads, sit at a corner and be silent and still and listen intently to the wind. Pay attention. If you hear words in the wind, take note, for the winds at the crossroads speak of the most important things that will occur during the upcoming year.

· EXERCISE 20 ·

Double Cross Windowsill Spell

Is it a coincidence that the double cross also looks just like the Celtic Ogham symbol for gorse, also known as furze or broom? The yellow-flowered furze was used in Wales to magically protect the home against the dangers of roaming fae and negative spells, hexes, or general negative energy.

A double cross looks like a lowercase "t" with two crossbars instead of one. In Christian tradition this is sometimes called a patriarchal cross or Cross of Lorraine. Whether you think of it as the Ogham gorse or Cross of Lorraine, both are symbols for spiritual protection from baneful forces.

Simply draw the symbol in red ink on a small piece of paper and draw a circle around it. Place one on each windowsill of your home to act as a shield from any roaming negative energies of any form that may be roaming throughout the land on Halloween.

· EXERCISE 21 ·

Parshell Protection Talisman

This tradition is so old that many of the Irish who create these talismans every year on Halloween have long forgotten where the tradition comes from or what the words even mean, but this folk custom carries on. A parshell is quite easy to make. I made my first one this year on Halloween, and it's very simple but packed with magic and tradition.

According to the legend, this talisman must be made only on Halloween, and you make a new one every year on Halloween to replace the one from the previous year. When the old one comes down, you are supposed to shout "Fonstarensheehy!"

What does that mean? Some suggest that it's a phonetic interpretation of a word, although it's probably a phrase that relates to warding against the fey folk, which this amulet is supposed to protect against, as well as bad luck, illness, and all forms of malevolent spirits.

You'll need two sticks about six to seven inches long; I used two that had fallen from my oak tree. The other thing you'll need is straw, rushes, or some other kind of string-like plant material. I used raffia; while definitely not traditional, it actually worked great. Hold both sticks together, side by side, and tie them together right in the middle with one end of the raffia. Pull the sticks into the form of an X and then tie them again across the sticks in the opposite way. Now begin wrapping the raffia around the crossed sticks, going in a clockwise direction and weaving over one stick and under the next, and keep going in this manner.

Keep going until you end up with a disk of woven raffia in the center of the crossed sticks, and the sticks are about halfway covered. Then tie the end to the stick in a triple knot and create a loop to hang it from. That's all there is to it!

Now you have a traditional Irish Halloween talisman to protect you from all sorts of ailments. According to custom, it's hung up over the door on the inside and left there all year until next Halloween, when you make a new one. Some people keep the old one the guard their barn or garage, or you can burn or bury it, returning it to the realm of spirit.

Don't forget to shout "Fonstarensheehy!" when you change them out. What will happen if you don't? I'm not going to be the one to find out.

Needfire Warding and Good Luck Spell

During medieval times, Halloween bonfires were lit with the belief that they would guard against malevolent witchcraft and the plague. This tradition was, of course, a holdover from Samhain bonfires and ancient magical traditions of the needfire. The kindling of a needfire is an old practice, a special kind of fire used by shepherds to ward off disease or hard times in general. Often these fires were ritually used at Beltane and Samhain. We usually have a bonfire on Samhain night, but we don't follow the old tradition of rubbing sticks together because we're terrible at it.

There were also nine trees associated with a magical fire. It's difficult to get a log from all nine of these trees since these days most people have smaller yards with fewer sources of firewood. I've devised a charm to use while lighting a Halloween needfire to maintain the intention of the needfires of old but still be practical for modern Halloween celebrations. We don't have the plague around here, so it must be working.

You don't have to have an open field to enjoy a need-fire. Many people sit outside on Halloween with a fire in their chiminea, metal fire pit, or grill. Gather as many bits of the following nine trees as you can: alder chips (such as for BBQ), a hazelnut, oak twig or leaf, a bit of birch bark, etc. If you can't get all nine, it's okay; just get as many as possible. On a piece of brown paper—a piece of grocery bag will do—write the names of all nine sacred woods: birch, rowan, ash, alder, willow, hawthorn, oak, holly, hazel. Wrap all the bits of tree that you have gathered up as tight as you can, and add it to your kindling before you start your fire.

Say this charm to set your intention right before you start the fire:

> *I kindle this needfire with nine spirits of wood*
> *A flame guarding us from all harm and for good*
> *May this fire kindle brightly on All Hallows' Eve*
> *Blessing us as we want, blessing us as we need.*

As you enjoy the fire, consider grabbing a dry leaf off the ground and naming it for whatever you want to banish from your life in the coming year: a bad habit, situation, or obstacle that's holding you back are all good choices. Fill it with thoughts of what you want gone from your life and then cast it into your fire.

If you live where you can't do a needfire, you can use a candle in a similar way to bless and ward your home. Write the names of the nine woods and place them under a candle. If you've gathered bits of the nine trees, simply place them around the candle and use the charm as you light it. Don't burn leaves in the house, of course, but you can write what you wish to banish on a slip of paper, light it from the candle, and carefully burn it in a fire-proof dish.

• EXERCISE 23 •
Blessing Your Borders

Halloween is a time of thresholds and borders. Vandals used to remove gates and border markers, sometimes leaving a jack-o'-lantern to infer the mischief was made by spirits or faeries. There were customs of walking the borders of properties to bless them yearly with the children in tow to make sure they were aware of the borders, driving the point home to stay away from properties that were not theirs.

Here is a spell to bless and spiritually reinforce the borders of your property; this is a good one to use outside along your property or fence line. All you need for this one is a lit jack-o'-lantern, either of the pumpkin or turnip variety. As you walk the border, your jack-o'-lantern will act as an emissary between the worlds. As you show him the borders and bless the boundary lines, you're asking your jack-o'-lantern to communicate your request for the protection of your property from the spirits of the land.

Starting in the east, turn your jack-o'-lantern to face toward the border as you say:

> *Jack of the light, will o' the wisp bright*
> *Spirits of the land here on All Hallows' Night*
> *Behold ye my borders to bless and to keep*
> *Whether working, playing, or fast asleep.*

Walk clockwise along the property, repeating the charm at each corner or landmark until you've made it all the way around to where you started.

If you're performing this one outside along your borders and you have nosy neighbors, you can just be casual; carry your pumpkin under your arm as if you're looking for just the right spot to display him and recite the charm under your breath or even in your head. If you prefer, just do it inside your living space, walking along the outer walls of the home and pausing at doors and windows to recite the charm.

Your jack-o'-lantern can act as an emissary between the worlds.

Scottish Charm for Ghoulies and Ghosties

Back when I was in grade school, I first read this short passage in a book of scary stories and poems. I just loved it when I read it, and I felt that it had some significance; instinctively, I memorized it just in case I needed it. It seemed like the kind of thing that could be helpful if there was something under the bed, in the closet, or if your music box began playing all by itself for no reason at all and you couldn't move a muscle because you were so freaked out—yeah, *that* kind of thing.

As it turns out, while you might call it an incantation or charm of protection, it was first written down as a traditional Scottish saying or prayer, and while I just love the whimsical, antiquated wording, no one seems to know its origins. I have many other incantations, some written down and some memorized over the years, but I've never forgotten this one. Does it work, you might ask? Well, that music box stopped playing and the energy in the room lightened up after it was spoken!

Since I perceive deity as being both male and female, as in the forms of the God and Goddess, I now use "Good Lord and Lady" instead of just "Good Lord" from the original version, but either version works.

From ghoulies and ghosties
And long-leggedy beasties
And things that go bump in the night,
Good Lord (and Lady) deliver us.

• EXERCISE 25 •

Turnip Jack-o'-Lantern Guardian Spell

This is a version of a popular spell that I wrote for the month of October in *Llewellyn's 2012 Spell-A-Day Almanac*. It draws on the origins of the jack-o'-lantern as a form of spiritual protection against unfriendly spirits. This spell was originally written for a pumpkin jack-o'-lantern, but I decided to give you a turnip version here to hearken back to the original jack-o'-lantern. If you're intrigued by the old tradition of a turnip jack-o'-lantern, as I was, take a look at exercise 3 for instructions on finding the right turnip and carving your turnip jack-o'-lantern.

Use this simple protection spell to install a guardian at your door. Procure a large turnip—they should be in stores in October—and place it near your front door, either inside or outside. Draw a small pentagram on the bottom of the turnip or pumpkin with a pencil; it will etch lightly into the skin of the turnip. Hold your turnip up to the moon and repeat the following:

Treasured turnip, watch over my home
Protecting from bane all you behold
By the power of this root in the pale moonlight
Shield us from harm both day and night.

Leave your enchanted turnip as a watchful guardian. Finish the spell by carving it a few days before Halloween and lighting it up on Halloween night.

• EXERCISE 26 •

Honor Your Ancestors

Many people set up a shelf or table for Samhain or Halloween as a special place of honor and a solemn remembrance of those we love who have crossed over into the realm of spirit. Some traditions choose to remember those who have passed from the material realm over the past year and can include family, friends, or anyone who has had an impact on their lives. Other traditions include ancestors from generations ago or people from history that mean something to them. We also see this practice as an integral part of the celebration of Día de los Muertos in Mexican custom to guide the spirits to the altar and represent the temporary nature of life.

This is a beautiful way to focus on the spiritual aspect of the season. You can set up a shelf anywhere you like with photos, memorabilia, candles, and flowers, celebrating the beloved dead. The area should be kept clean and neat and should be a place where people don't generally toss their keys or set down a cup of coffee; it should be a space reserved for spirit. If you leave flowers in a vase, change the water often. You can choose roses to represent love and blessings, marigolds as in the Mexican custom, or favorite flowers of someone special that you're honoring. Another nice addition is to display a loved one's favorite sweets, candy, or drink.

Feast for the Dead

Another custom for remembering the dead on Halloween is a special feast known as a dumb supper. Dumb suppers were often prepared and eaten in silence, leaving a full plate for the beloved dead who may happen by on Halloween night. This is a beautiful tradition, and I honestly wish that I could manage to cook a meal in complete silence. I'm sure my family does too since I often talk to myself while I work, listen to music, and, yes, sometimes I sing. Cooking is joyful to me, and I just can't help it. In addition, my family sure can't manage to stay silent on Halloween, so the legit dumb supper has never happened at my house. Does that make me a bad witch? No way—just a loud, merry one!

In my family we do, however, celebrate by offering a feast for our beloved dead. We figure if our house was silent, they might think they had the wrong address anyway. We prepare a plate of food for the passing spirits on the good china; we usually set it at a small table in the garden so that the spirits may be undisturbed if they stop by. Some people prefer to leave food offerings near photos of their ancestors somewhere in the home. If you leave food offerings for your beloved dead on Halloween, it is believed that their spirit will enjoy the essence of the food and the loving spirit in which it is offered while the physical food itself will remain. The food from such offerings after Halloween can be enjoyed by the family with a toast to the spirits or, alternately, left somewhere in nature (being sure to remove any non-biodegradables, of course).

• EXERCISE 28 •
Halloween Prosperity Spell

Halloween/Samhain is the witches' New Year, and that means it's a great time to work some quick prosperity magic. It's a harvest festival, so this spell awakens abundance and prosperity into your life. We can all use that!

Carve a simple spider on top of an orange tealight candle with a pin; make sure it has eight legs. Sprinkle it with cinnamon and basil. Surround the candle with four coins of equal value and four pumpkin seeds, point-side facing in; alternate the coins and seeds. As you light the candle, say:

No tricks and all treats
This spell shall unfold
The year ahead brings in
Silver and gold.

Let the candle burn down. Eat the four pumpkin seeds at midnight. Tuck the four coins in your wallet (separate from your other coins), and don't spend them all year.

five

HALLOWEEN DIVINATION AND SPIRIT COMMUNICATION

Divination work and Halloween go hand in hand; after all, this specific season of the witch is a great hinge of the year. The Celts knew this, and that's why Samhain was recognized as the New Year in their tradition. During big psychic shifts in energy—like the shift we feel around Halloween—it is a perfect time to look forward, backward, and even beyond. They say the veil between the world of the living and the realm of spirit is at its thinnest now, so we may peer into worlds normally unavailable to us.

In the Celtic lands, the faerie mounds were places where the troupes of otherworldly beings might pour through the gateways made available to them as the hinge of time creaked just a bit. People worried that revenant spirits might come through the cracks and wreak havoc on their lives, but at the same time they hoped for precious signs or even communication from their beloved family and friends who had made their transitions from the mortal realm. These beliefs set the scene for a tradition of practicing many methods of divination on or around the cross-quarter between the autumn equinox and the winter solstice.

The art of divination during Halloween has been documented across cultures, religions, and status. Old or young, rich or poor, pious or Pagan, we all want some extra information to help us make the best decisions that we can as we move forward. Halloween is that time of the year when we have license to peek into the beyond and ask what the future holds.

It all seems very mysterious and daunting if you've never tried it. But really, there is a theory that everyone has psychic abilities to a certain extent and that we need only exercise those areas of our brains to be able to know things that we can't perceive with our other senses. Yes, some people are naturals: psychics, intuitives, mediums; but by using the tools of the trade, we can all give it a try and maybe even discover that we have a knack for it as well.

Throughout history people have stretched their psychic muscles on and around Halloween for a very good reason: if you have a bit of hidden talent in that area, Halloween is one of the most promising times to try it out because it's the best energetic environment for such activities. Learning to ski in the summer would be a challenge since there's no snow, but on a snowy winter day it's the perfect time to take advantage of the seasonal environment to explore winter sports. So it makes sense to explore psychic knowledge during the time that it's most available to us.

Many of these methods were considered parlor games, especially during the popularity of the philosophy of Spiritualism, which had long flourished in Europe and began to gain traction in the United States in the mid 1800s, when having psychic parties was all the rage, especially on Halloween. At the time, many adherents to this philosophy found that it worked fine with the dogma of the Christian churches they attended, so holding a séance or

Throughout history people have stretched their psychic muscles on and around Halloween for a very good reason: if you have a bit of hidden talent in that area, Halloween is one of the most promising times to try it out because it's the best energetic environment for such activities.

having your palm read was not only acceptable but considered a great reason to have a party on a Saturday night. First Ladies of the United States Jane Pierce and Mary Todd Lincoln were among the first to hold séances in the White House. Both had tragically lost young sons and sought out psychics to connect with them again.

Communication with the dead or seeking extrasensory information was commonplace and wasn't seen as unusual at all. Perhaps the combination of the large numbers of people lost to war and disease combined with more available knowledge about science made communities feel a need to reach out while being a bit less threatened by the supernatural.

The people of the late 1800s found that on the heels of the ages of reason and enlightenment, they were moving into the modern era, which could still hold some mysteries to explore with a clear head and both feet firmly in this world. People wanted to believe in the spirit world, and with a foundation in philosophy to steady their nerves, they were bravely exploring the esoteric.

Which Way Does the Wind Blow?

There is an old agricultural divination practice done on Halloween that hearkens back to a time when people's ability to survive was in the hands of nature's whims. Farmers used to carry a candle into the garden on Halloween to see which way the wind was blowing. The direction of the wind that night would foretell of the prevailing wind for the next three months.

To learn what way the wind is blowing in your financial situation, write down four possible sources of income, one on each of the four corners of a piece of paper; put it in a large bowl or cauldron and set a candle in the middle. Walk with the bowl, candle, and paper down to your garden or to the very back of your property. Watch the candle flame: it will point to the best source of income for you to pursue over the next several months.

Divination, séances, and spirit communication became so in vogue that by the 1920s many unscrupulous frauds began using stage magic tricks in order to create theatrical séances and psychic readings, swindling many of their trusting clients and unfortunately tarnishing the reputation of the time-honored art of divination.

There were so many frauds that stage magician and escape artist Harry Houdini dedicated quite a bit of time during the last years of his life debunking fake psychics until his death on Halloween in 1926. Houdini, although a skeptic, held on to the hope that spirits could send messages and even arranged a secret code with his wife, Bess, that he would attempt to pass on to her after his death. To this day people hold séances in attempts to contact Harry Houdini on Halloween night, the anniversary of his death. Incidentally, the only recording of Houdini's voice was made the day before Halloween in 1914 on Edison wax cylinders.

The popularity of divination among the general public continued on through the '50s and '60s, and while the practice has ebbed and flowed a bit with the general public, many have kept the practices going. Today Halloween is a popular time to get a tarot or oracle deck reading, cast runes, or use a pendulum. Some people consider working with divination or spirit communication on Halloween entertaining, but it also can be an enlightening way to look at the energies that surround you, discover the unseen, and look at where you've been in life—and where you're going.

• EXERCISE 29 •

How to Use Pendulums

Pendulums are a really easy way to do a little Halloween divination; anyone can use one. I have a lovely crystal pendulum that I use for quick yes or no–type situations. Pendulums can be made of metal, wood, carved stone, or other materials. Owning and using a nice pendulum is a real treat. But if you want to try one, you don't need to spend a lot of money. You can make one easily on the fly from simple household items; it's basically a weight on a string or chain.

I have a couple versions for you. The first one is an old folk magic trick I've seen used frequently at baby showers. Someone would string a piece of the mother-to-be's hair through her wedding ring, then suspend it over her baby bump; if it swung in a circle, that meant it's a girl; back and forth meant it was a boy. I hardly see this one used these days because almost everyone has ultrasounds done now. A simple pendulum like this can be made in the same fashion to use for yes-no questions as well. I've done it many times when I was out of the house or couldn't find my actual pendulum, so I just used a ring. This one is perfect for a Halloween party because it's so easy. You can use a piece of your hair (if your hair is long) or use a lightweight chain or string to thread the ring through.

Another easy way to make your own pendulum is with a cork and a needle and thread. Carefully press the point of the needle into the end of the cork, as close as you can get to the center, and then thread the needle with about 10 inches of thread. Knot the two ends together.

I hold the end of the string between my index finger and thumb, with my elbow resting on the table so that the pendulum can swing freely. I ask the pendulum, "Show me yes," and it will swing in a certain way (for me, usually in a circle). Then I ask, "Show me no," and it will swing differently (for me, usually back and forth). Then I ask,

191

five

"Show me unknown"; for me, the pendulum slows and nearly stops. I call this calibrating my pendulum. Different people will get different responses when calibrating, just make note of what works for you. There's no right or wrong in this case, just be sure that you know which kind of swing represents each response.

Now you can ask any question and watch the pendulum for answers. This is some easy and fun divination that you can whip up anywhere on the fly and definitely at your next Halloween party.

• EXERCISE 30 •

It's in the Cards

Tarot is probably the most popular form of divination on Halloween or anytime of the year for that matter, but many people who've never had a reading or done readings themselves try it on Halloween. Whether you're new to tarot or have some experience, tarot goes with Halloween like chocolate goes with peanut butter: a perfect pairing.

If you're new to tarot and want to do readings for yourself or friends on Halloween, you should start looking for a deck at some point before Halloween so that you have a chance to familiarize yourself with it a bit.

There are lots to choose from; as a tarot and oracle deck designer myself, I'll tell you not all decks are for everyone. Choose one that speaks to you, makes you feel comfortable, and inspires you when you look at it. You can look up images of decks online; some metaphysical bookstores have sample decks you can browse through. There are some pretty cool tarot and oracle decks with Halloween themes or you might like a witch, vampire, or ghost-themed deck for Halloween readings. If you're an experienced reader, Halloween might be a fun time to explore a new deck with one of these motifs. I just discovered a gorgeous Halloween oracle deck that I have my eye on. A word of warning: once you have your first deck, finding new ones can become very addictive!

For those who don't know the difference between tarot decks and oracle decks, it's pretty simple. Tarot decks generally have seventy-eight cards and are organized similarly to playing cards. Oracle decks usually have fewer cards than tarot decks, and they're often each organized in their own unique ways. Whether you want to start with a tarot deck or oracle deck is up to you. Oracle decks can be used in pretty much the same way that tarot decks can. There are entire books published about how to read tarot cards, so this is just the tip of the iceberg. As you learn, you might want to seek out one or two of those books. Most good decks come with their own handbook to get you started. I'll give you a basic overview on doing card readings for Halloween.

First, come up with an appropriate question to ask. The questioner can ask a yes-no question, ask about the best course of action to achieve a goal, focus on a decision that needs to be made, or even just request a general reading to see what's going on around you. No matter what the question, you should keep it foremost in your mind while shuffling the cards. As you focus on the question, shuffle the cards so that the cards come up at random. Generally, you shuffle until you feel it is right.

Lay out the cards in a pattern called a spread. The book that comes with your deck should have a few spreads to guide you. When you're interpreting cards for a reading, it's fine to listen to your intuition in addition to the card meanings. Some readers might get a different feeling from a card than what the books say; trust yourself and allow the cards to speak to you. Trusting your intuition is part of embracing the energies of Samhain and Halloween as you do your readings.

If you're at a smaller gathering
and want to get more in depth,
a great Halloween layout is
the twelve-month spread. It's
perfect for getting a glimpse
at the upcoming year. Starting
at the top, lay out twelve cards
in a circle. The top card is the
card representing November,
then just go clockwise around
the circle. Each card is a month
until you come back around
to October of the next year.

You can set the mood by using a Halloween-themed cloth to lay your cards out on—moons for mysticism and the unseen, spiderwebs as a symbol of connectivity to all things, skulls to connect us to the power of our ancestors. If you're just having fun and want to do quick readings for a lot of people, I suggest just doing a quick three-card reading: three cards in a row from left to right that represent past, present, and future. You can also let your friends take a photo of their reading with their phone for later reference.

Experienced readers, here's a cool exercise to do on Halloween/Samhain with another tarot-reading friend. Each of you should shuffle your deck while focusing on the same question for the same querent, and then do the same spread. I've done this exercise with witch friends while trying to iron out a big problem, and the results can be very interesting indeed. This exercise offers a multidimensional reading and big confirmations as well.

The Misunderstood Ouija Board

My teenage son Tristan and I recently watched an episode of *I Love Lucy* that included a séance and numerology; even a Ouija board was mentioned without controversy or fear about invoking demons. When exactly did the Ouija board shift from being a popular Halloween curiosity and pastime, practiced by the social elite and working class alike, to becoming feared and maligned as a gateway to spiritual danger?

It was well after Halloween but during the dark half of the year, in December 1973, when *The Exorcist* premiered in theaters. I remember it well because I loved scary movies, but I was way too young to see it. Basically, it did for Ouija boards what *Psycho* did for enjoying a peaceful shower or what *Jaws* did to a day at the beach. In the film, Regan, a twelve-year-old girl, messes around with a Ouija board and becomes possessed by a demon. The film frightened people so much that suddenly our culture was now terrified of a piece of masonite with a picture on it and a plastic triangle sold in the toy aisle. Even today there are some experienced magical practitioners who work with divination tools such as tarot or scrying mirrors on a regular basis but still harbor fears of the Ouija or other talking boards, not even realizing that those fears stem from popular culture and not real metaphysics.

I was a particularly imaginative child during the 1970s. My friends and I used a Ouija board frequently on Halloween nights and at sleepovers, so my own family picked one up. My mom and dad used it in a hotel on a trip to Roswell, New Mexico, where my dad was exhibiting in an art gallery there. They asked for the initials of the first person who would buy a painting from my dad at the exhibit, and it proved correct in its reply the next day. Did that plastic triangle summon up a demon who was moonlighting as an art agent? I really doubt it.

According to the instructions, two people are supposed to sit across from each other with their fingers lightly resting (and this is the key: *very* lightly) on the planchette, and then you concentrate and simply ask the question in general. The planchette will sometimes glide slowly across the board and point to letters or numbers to indicate a response. As a witchy woman, I bet you expected me to tell you that a spirit is moving it, didn't you? Well, I don't think that is the case. I actually agree with the scientific theory that the movement is caused by a phenomenon known as the ideomotor response, tapping into our subconscious mind and creating automatic yet imperceptible muscle movements in our fingertips, moving the planchette across the board.

A group of scientists decided to study the phenomenon's connection with the subconscious mind after watching college students use a Ouija board at a Halloween party. The studies they did and later published suggested that when people are using the board, they appear to be answering through their own subconscious mind without even knowing it. In one part of the study, blindfolded players were told that another person was playing across from them even though they were playing alone, and many of them reported after the experiment that the "other person" had moved the planchette. This showed that the movement was completely subconscious. So the question "Did you move it?" is totally well-founded, but not in the way you thought.

Does that mean it's not a valid form of divination? From a metaphysical standpoint, it may prove that it *is*

divination! If we are subconsciously moving the planch-ette, then our own subconscious mind is answering the questions.

It's a widely held theory among the metaphysical com-munity that everyone has some psychic abilities; some people use them all the time, others are buried more deeply, but they are there. Simply put, your subconscious mind is tapping into the astral, then using the board as a tool to access the answers, and what better time to do that than on Halloween, when we have more access to the astral? When you know that, it's no longer scary nor demonic, but it can be a tool for reaching into our own extrasensory abilities.

A Ouija board can be a tool for reaching into our own extrasensory abilities.

As for anecdotal reports of scary things happening, yep, that's the power of the subconscious mind. If you've decided that it will be a scary or dangerous experience, then you've put the energy of that into the astral and also into your own subconscious. Honestly, if you can't banish the idea of demons working through the Ouija board, you shouldn't use it because you're just going to have your own psychic fears leaking out and wreaking havoc, just like people who are nervous about chainsaws should probably not use them to cut wood. However, if you can manage to put it in perspective, it can be a positive experience, and you might even gain some extrasensory information.

Now that you know how it works, here's how to use a Ouija board (or any other version of a talking board) without fear at your next Halloween get-together. You might want to use the grounding and centering technique in lucky exercise 13 and the shield of light just for good measure in exercise 14. Light some candles and incense or a sage bundle to set the mood and bless your space. You could even set a jack-o'-lantern nearby to guard over your space since they traditionally keep any curious baneful spirits away. If you wish, you may use an opening statement to bless the space such as:

This space is filled with only positive energy
as we peek through the veil on Halloween night
seeking answers to our questions.
We call upon the power of the subconscious mind
to speak through this board.
This space is blessed and protected.

Once you are calm and in a good state of mind, each person should rest their fingertips very lightly on the edges of the planchette so that their fingers are barely in contact with it; this helps the ideomotor response to work. Then simply ask a question. Don't ask the "ghost or spirit of the board" or anything like that, just ask the question out loud. Remember: you are tapping into your own psychic subconscious mind, not summoning a demon.

It can be helpful to write down the questions and answers, too, so that you can refer to them later. Just try to relax and let it do its thing. When the session has ended, if you wish to clear the emotionally and psychically charged energy of the room, you can do that by smudging with sage or waving incense smoke through the room or even ringing a bell. You can also close the session with a statement such as this:

> *We now close the doors that communicate through*
> *the subconscious. We thank our own higher powers*
> *for helping us interact with the astral realm as we*
> *now return our minds to the mundane world.*

When you're done, pass the board and planchette through sage or incense smoke just to neutralize the energies. Last, grab a snack; it's one of the easiest ways to bring your mind back to this world.

If you decide to try using a Ouija or any other talking board alone, you can do so without any danger, so feel free to try it if you wish. The reason they suggest two (or sometimes more) people is that it just works better that way, and that was reflected in the study that was done.

• EXERCISE 32 •
Tea Leaf Readings

For me, tea leaf readings conjure up the image of a simple cottage table by a blazing hearth, a slice of warm barm-brak, a cup of tea full of mysteries, and a wise woman patiently awaiting your last sip so that she can read the map of your life in its leavings—and on All Hallows' Eve, of course. It feels very Old World because, of course, it is. A classic folk divination technique, reading tea leaves— also known as tasseography—requires a creative mind, a cup and saucer, and some loose tea. Are you the kind of person who is patient, with an eye for details? Do you see shapes in the clouds? If so, you might be pretty good at reading tea leaves. Give it a try on Halloween; whether reading for yourself or someone else, it should be an interesting experience.

A large shallow teacup works best, plain white inside with no distracting patterns. You'll need a saucer to turn the cup over onto. Many of us these days drink out of large straight-sided mugs, and these are great for a big cup of tea but useless for tea leaf reading. If you don't own a proper teacup and saucer, you don't have to spend a lot: check out your local secondhand shop. Get one with a wide, round opening and angled sides instead of straight sides.

Now for the tea: don't go ripping open a tea bag like I did the first time I tried tea reading, as that tea is ground way too fine to use for a decent reading. Pick up some loose tea—a good midrange-priced black, green, or oolong tea works well. As long as it's a broad-leafed tea and not fine and powdery, any tea will work.

To brew a single cup, put on the kettle and put a teaspoon of loose tea in your cup. When the water comes to a boil, turn it off and let it sit for one minute, then pour it into the teacup. Let it steep for five minutes while you think about your question and the tea leaves absorb liquid. You may add a bit of sweetener of your choice but no cream because it can cause the leaves to stick together.

You or the person you're doing the reading for can now enjoy the cup of tea. When there's about a teaspoon of liquid left in the cup, place a napkin on your saucer. The questioner should hold the teacup by the handle in their left hand and focus on a question while gazing into the cup. Swirl the tea around in the cup counterclockwise, then turn the cup upside down onto the saucer and leave it there for about a minute while the tea drains away. Now you can turn your cup over; what pictures do you see? Pick up the cup and really examine it.

A few things to know:

- The leaves near the rim represent things that will happen soon.

- The leaves near the bottom of the cup are in the distant future (usually about a year).

- The rest of the leaves fall in the middle time-wise.

- Pictures nearer the handle will affect the questioner most directly.

- Watch for anything that you recognize as a picture.

- Pay attention to groupings and how the images interact with each other.

There are more symbols and their meanings than I have room for in this little book, but you can easily find online tea leaf dictionaries if you want to find out what specific symbols mean.

There are a few that come up frequently:

Anchor: good luck, prosperity

Bird: flying means positive news, sitting means success and achievement

Boat: letting go of what doesn't serve you or
    refuge from strife

Butterfly: transformation, success

Circle: money, presents, or a ring

Clover: good luck

Crescent moon: success and happiness

Dog: friendship, loyalty, but also look at the
    stance

Fish: good news

Heart: love in all its forms

Human figure or face: look at the expression of
    the stance or face for cues

Letters: usually an initial of a person or possibly
    a place

Line: a journey; unbroken is good progress,
    broken means some roadblocks

Numbers: can represent timing, days of the week,
    or month

Square: trapped, boxed in; watch for trouble

• • • •

Have fun with it and take your time. Open your imagination on Halloween and see what the tea leaves have to tell you about in the upcoming witches' New Year.

TIP 11
Auguring on Halloween

Halloween or the first Monday after Halloween is a favorable time of the year to perform a simple ritual known as the frith to determine what the upcoming year has in store. Right before sunrise, make your way to the front door in bare feet. Close your eyes. Open the door and stand in the doorway with each hand on either side of the door jam. Now set an intention in your mind to make the unseen visible and to see something that will be enlightening about the future. When you open your eyes, pay close attention to everything you see before you, making note of good or bad omens. You can look up what you see in a dream dictionary to see what they symbolize.

• EXERCISE 33 •
How to Host a Séance

This is the ultimate Halloween spirit work. For this method of spiritual communication, all you need is a quiet room, a few friends, candles, incense, and an open heart. Holding a séance on Halloween is a time-honored tradition, and while it is actually a much more subtle and nuanced experience than you'll see in movies, it can be very moving for the people involved. If you want to try this, I will share with you a method of doing it respectfully and safely so that it can be a good experience for everyone involved.

Decide on your guest list; this kind of thing isn't for everyone. A serious approach and positive state of mind are really preferred; people with a negative attitude about the whole thing or people who are terrified will bring that fearful energy to the séance, which can affect the outcome of the experience for everyone. Basically, this isn't the exercise for anyone who's overly distressed by Ouija boards or even the idea of ghosts.

Find a Happy Medium

Now think about who you might want to communicate with from the other side of the veil between the worlds. Some people who host a séance might reach out to any benevolent spirits who want to communicate, while others are looking for communication with someone specific. If you're reaching out to a specific person, consider including a photo on the table, perhaps their favorite food or drink, or softly play music they appreciated.

Unless you've hired a professional medium or psychic clairvoyant to lead your séance, choose the person in your group who is most psychic to lead the séance. We all have that friend—the one who has a certain amount of psychic abilities, strong intuition, and can sense the vibe in a room, who isn't afraid of cemeteries, and who can command attention; that's your person. Everyone there will add to the energy, but your group leader will be the one to offer a blessing, invite and say farewell to presences, and serve as a barometer for the psychic energy during the séance, so this person should be both rock solid and open to energies.

Set the Tone

Have a quiet, clean area with a table or circle on the floor, a spread-out tablecloth or floor mat, a grouping of candles, and perhaps a few crystals, if you have them, to boost the energy. It's Halloween, so why not include a few turnip jack-o'-lanterns (exercise 3) to ward away dark energies and invite spirits of the beloved dead? The mini pumpkin tealight holders from exercise 5 would be very appropriate too!

It's a good idea to smudge the room by wafting the air with a burning bundle of sage or incense, or spraying the air lightly with a water bottle filled with water and a few drops of essential oils such as sandalwood or frankincense. This cleanses and blesses the energy of the room. A limited amount of good-hearted humor as you prepare is okay, but people should keep a general attitude of respect and decorum. I know, everyone wants to take selfies or pictures of the table with candles and crystals, just be sure to do them before or after (not during) the séance.

Before you begin, make sure everyone turns off their phones. If you're using one or more to record the event, make sure they're on silent. Phones are a distraction, and the participants need to focus their attention on the communication at hand. It's also a good idea to lead the group in grounding and centering (see exercise 13) and the shield of light exercise (exercise 14).

Cast a circle around the area by holding hands to create a circuit. Visualize the area around the table being surrounded in a sphere of white light, and make sure all participants know that contact with each other's hands should be kept in order to keep the energy steady. If hands are dropped, nothing bad will happen, but the delicate energy that opens the lines of communication with the spirit realm may dissipate, ending everything early.

Reach Across the Veil

Dim the lights and light the candles. The group leader can now open up communication by making a statement with positive intention, such as:

> *This space is blessed and protected as we call upon only benevolent spirits to reach out to us across the thin veil this Halloween night. We are open to messages from those who communicate only for our greater good as we respectfully entreat the energies that once walked this earth in material form to contact us here in this blessed space.*

You don't have to use these words exactly, but this gives you the idea; it should be positive, respectful, specific, and inviting only spirits of the departed. At this point, a specific person may be named if you wish.

Everyone should bring along realistic expectations of the evening. Communication during a séance will probably not be what you've seen in the movies or on TV. There won't be furniture flying around the room, and the walls won't bleed; a great deal of holding a séance is waiting quietly for a feeling or a flicker of the candle flame. It's very likely that your communication will come in the form of a feeling, visions, or a voice in your head. Don't expect a full ghostly apparition to appear. People will be more likely to sense their presence in other ways, sometimes in the way that you can feel someone watching you; you can feel their energy in the room. If you're really lucky, you might get a few more obvious signs like a thump, a temperature change, or candle flames reacting oddly.

People may ask questions and "feel" for a response. If your group leader is experienced at spirit communication, they may be able to verbalize the messages from the group. Another method is to simply ask for a sign, such as candle flickers for a yes response to a yes-no question. Communicate respectfully and be sure to treat spirits as honored guests; after all, you invited them, and their trip to get there was probably the most challenging of all your guests.

Damage Control

If at any point anyone in the group feels uncomfortable or afraid, you may have an uninvited spirit who popped by. If you get a spiritual guest that seems angry or unpleasant, there's no point in letting it get the better of you. We've all been to parties when a guest misbehaved and made everyone feel uncomfortable, and this is no different— they were human once too, and humans aren't always nice and friendly. The group leader, now taking on the role of bouncer, should respond and send them packing with a firm, authoritative statement, something like:

> *No malevolent spirits are welcomed in this sacred space; only spirits aligned with our greater good may remain. The unwelcomed must now immediately depart back to your own realm, harming none along the way!*

Usually everyone should then feel the energy change as the annoying spirit makes their exit. If the bothersome guest won't leave, just end the séance and use the incense, sage, or spritz to clear the room again.

Closing Time

To close the séance, the leader should make a statement to let any spirits present know that the communication is now at an end and they should depart back to their own realm, using a statement like the following:

> *Thank you, good spirits, for joining us*
> *on Halloween evening. It is now time for you*
> *to journey back to your place beyond the veil.*
> *We sincerely thank you and honor the time*
> *we've spent together; hail and farewell.*
> *As the spirits depart, the door between*
> *the worlds closes, returning this*
> *space to the physical realm.*

The statement doesn't have to be this exactly but should include a thank you, a statement that all should depart, a farewell, and a closing of the door. Now everyone can release their hands and bring up the lights. Blow out the candles. You may wish to cleanse the space again the way you did before you began. Everyone can compare their experiences, have a snack to return to normal reality, and think about the ways that Halloween brings us gifts of spirit and magic in many unexpected ways.

CONCLUSION

Halloween has always been filled with mystery and wonder. The thing about this celebration is that shedding light upon its history and practices does nothing to take the enchantment away from it; if anything, I think it deepens it.

Halloween is a time to celebrate our inner hopes and laugh at our fears. We feast on delicious bounty and indulge in sweets to our hearts' content. We can also raise

Feel the magic in the air—feel it with everything that you are. It's a peculiar sort of night; after all, you've always known it was more than masks and chocolate bars, so why not embrace Halloween for all that it is and be glad that it cast its spell on you?

a glass to our beloved dead and remember our ancestors who paved the way for us; all that we are and might become is fed by their very existence. We carve grinning faces in our pumpkins and fill our world with dancing skeletons and ethereal ghosts to bewitch our neighborhoods. We decide every year to transform ourselves for a night, becoming anyone we want to be as we step outside of ourselves.

Feel the magic in the air—feel it with everything that you are. It's a peculiar sort of night; after all, you've always known it was more than masks and chocolate bars, so why not embrace Halloween for all that it is and be glad that it cast its spell on you?

Now c'mon—grab your largest pillowcase. Let's go trick-or-treating!

Bibliography

Books

Danaher, Kevin. *The Year in Ireland: Irish Calendar Customs.* Cork: The Mercier Press, 1972.

Gauchou, Hélène L., Ronald A. Resink, and Sidney Fels. "Expression of Nonconcious Knowledge Via Ideomotor Actions," *Consciousness and Cognition*, volume 21, issue 2, June 2012.

Kelley, Ruth Edna. *The Book of Hallowe'en.* Norwood: Lothrop, Lee & Shepard, 1919. Kindle.

Matthews, John, and Caitlín Matthews. *The Element Encyclopedia of Magical Creatures.* London: Harper Element, 2005.

McNeill, F. Marian. *The Silver Bough, Volume 1* (Canongate Classic). Surrey: Stuart Titles, 2013. Kindle.

Morton, Lisa. *Trick-or-Treat: A History of Halloween.* London: Reaktion Books, 2012. Kindle.

Rajchel, Diana. *Samhain: Rituals, Recipes & Lore for Halloween.* Woodbury: Llewellyn, 2015.

Sayed, Deonna Kelli. *So You Want to Hunt Ghosts? A Down-to-Earth Guide.* Woodbury: Llewellyn, 2012.

Weschcke, Carl Llewellyn, and Joe. H. Slate. *All About Tea Leaf Reading.* Woodbury: Llewellyn, 2011. Kindle.

Online

"The Bat Diary: Find Out What Bats are Doing Throughout the Year." Acer Ecology. November 20, 2013. http://www.acerecology.co.uk/bat-diary/. Accessed 10/5/2017.

Black, Susa Morgan. "Deeper into Samhain." http://www.druidry.org/druid-way/teaching-and-practice/druid-festivals/samhain/deeper-samhain. Accessed 10/2/2017.

Kerr, Margee. "Why We Love to Be Scared." *Psychology Today*. October 7, 2015. https://www.psychologytoday.com/blog/why-we-scream/201510/why-we-love-be-scared. Accessed 10/21/2017.

McRobbie, Linda Rodriquez. "The Strange and Mysterious History of the Ouija Board." October 27, 2013. htpps://www.smithsonianmag.com/history/the-strange-and-mysterious-history-of-the-ouija-board-5860627/. Accessed 11/20/2017.

Mullally, Erin. "Samhain Revival: Looking for the Roots of Halloween in Ireland's Boyne Valley." November 1, 2016. https://www.archaeology.org/issues/232-1611/features/4940-ireland-halloween-roots#art_page2. Accessed 10/2/2017.

Nardone, Tom. "The Great Pumpkin Preservation Study: How To Preserve a Pumpkin Properly." http://www.extremepumpkins.com/pumpkin-preservation-methods.html. Accessed 10/12/2017.

Wiginton, Patti. "Samhain Folklore: Halloween Superstitions and Legends." August 28, 2016. https://www.thoughtco.com/samhain-folklore-and-superstitions-2562712. Accessed 10/6/2017.

GET MORE AT LLEWELLYN.COM

Visit us online to browse hundreds of our books and decks, plus sign up to receive our e-newsletters and exclusive online offers.

- Free tarot readings • Spell-a-Day • Moon phases
- Recipes, spells, and tips • Blogs • Encyclopedia
- Author interviews, articles, and upcoming events

GET SOCIAL WITH LLEWELLYN

Find us on f   🐦 @LlewellynBooks

www.Facebook.com/LlewellynBooks

GET BOOKS AT LLEWELLYN

LLEWELLYN ORDERING INFORMATION

Order online: Visit our website at www.llewellyn.com to select your books and place an order on our secure server.

Order by phone:
- Call toll free within the US at 1-877-NEW-WRLD (1-877-639-9753)
- We accept VISA, MasterCard, American Express, and Discover.
- Canadian customers must use credit cards.

Order by mail:
Send the full price of your order (MN residents add 6.875% sales tax) in US funds plus postage and handling to: Llewellyn Worldwide, 2143 Wooddale Drive, Woodbury, MN 55125-2989

POSTAGE AND HANDLING

STANDARD (US):
(Please allow 12 business days)
$30.00 and under, add $6.00.
$30.01 and over, FREE SHIPPING.

INTERNATIONAL ORDERS,
INCLUDING CANADA:
$16.00 for one book, plus $3.00 for
each additional book.

Visit us online for more shipping options.
Prices subject to change.

FREE CATALOG!

To order, call
1-877-
NEW-WRLD
ext. 8236
or visit our
website

To order, call 1-877-new-wrld or visit llewellyn.com

Prices subject to change without notice

Magical Dogs Tarot

MICKIE & DANIEL MUELLER

Dogs bring a special kind of magic into our lives with their boundless joy and unwavering loyalty. This charming tarot deck captures that magic, showcasing each dog's beauty, wisdom, and irresistible personality. *Magical Dogs Tarot* features delightful artwork and a variety of breeds, each facing the universal challenges, relationships, and life lessons that reveal the answers to our biggest questions. Organized by elemental suits—earth, sea, fire, and sky—and dog pack–inspired court cards, this deck transforms man's best friend into the tarot reader's perfect companion.

978-0-7387-5005-7

The Magical Dogs Tarot kit consists of a boxed set of 78 full-color cards and a 216-page book.

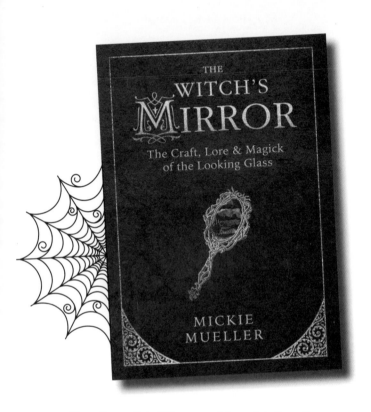

THE

WITCH'S
MIRROR

The Craft, Lore & Magick
of the Looking Glass

MICKIE
MUELLER

To order, call 1-877-new-wrld or visit llewellyn.com
Prices subject to change without notice

The Witch's Mirror

The Craft, Lore & Magick of the Looking Glass

MICKIE MUELLER

Discover the fascinating history, tradition, and modern uses of the witch's mirror. From choosing and making the perfect mirror to using it to boost self-esteem and prosperity, this book provides valuable information for witches of all levels. Fun and easy to use, *The Witch's Mirror* features advice from well-known witches as well as spells and crafts to enhance your magic.

Explore the symbols and practice of scrying, uncover the portrayals of mirrors in legends and pop culture, harness the reflective power of mirrors with meditations, and much more. Mickie Mueller invites you to gaze through the looking glass and see your magical self wielding the mirror as a key tool to a successful, happy, and enchanted life.

978-0-7387-4791-0

5 x 7 • 288 pages

To Write to the Author

If you wish to contact the author or would like more information about this book, please write to the author in care of Llewellyn Worldwide and we will forward your request. Both the author and the publisher appreciate hearing from you and learning of your enjoyment of this book and how it has helped you. Llewellyn Worldwide cannot guarantee that every letter written to the author can be answered, but all will be forwarded.

Please write to:

Mickie Mueller
℅ Llewellyn Worldwide
2143 Wooddale Drive
Woodbury, MN 55125-2989

Please enclose a self-addressed stamped envelope for reply
or $1.00 to cover costs. If outside the USA, enclose
an international postal reply coupon.

Many of Llewellyn's authors
have websites with additional
information and resources.
For more information,
please visit our website:

llewellyn.com